Escape *from* Leipzig

T0127673

Escape *from* Leipzig

Harald Fritzsch

University of Munich, Germany

Translated by K Heusch

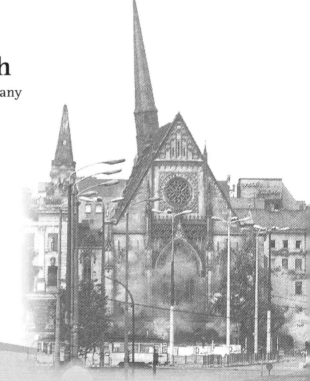

World Scientific

NEW JERSEY · LONDON · SINGAPORE · BEIJING · SHANGHAI · HONG KONG · TAIPEI · CHENNAI

Published by

World Scientific Publishing Co. Pte. Ltd.

5 Toh Tuck Link, Singapore 596224

USA office: 27 Warren Street, Suite 401-402, Hackensack, NJ 07601

UK office: 57 Shelton Street, Covent Garden, London WC2H 9HE

Library of Congress Cataloging-in-Publication Data
Fritzsch, Harald, 1943–
[Flucht aus Leipzig. English]
Escape from Leipzig / by H. Fritzsch ; translated by K. Heusch ; with a foreword
written by G. 't Hooft.
    p. cm.
   ISBN-13: 978-981-279-009-5 (hardcover : alk. paper)
   ISBN-10: 981-279-009-8 (hardcover : alk. paper)
   ISBN-13: 978-981-279-306-5 (paperback : alk. paper)
   ISBN-10: 981-279-306-2 (paperback : alk. paper)
   1. Germany (East)--Politics and government. 2. Fritzsch, Harald, 1943–
3. Escapes--Germany. 4. Political refugees--Germany. I. Heusch, Karin. II. Hooft, G. 't
III. Title.

DD287.4.F7513 2008
943'.1087092--dc22
[B]

                       2007044688

Flucht aus Leipzig
© 1990, 2004 (revised edition) by Piper Verlag GmbH, München.

British Library Cataloguing-in-Publication Data
A catalogue record for this book is available from the British Library.

Printed in Singapore.

In memory of my parents
Marianne and Erich Fritzsch

Foreword

Spread all over the globe, a group of scientists is engaged in the study of the highly complex mathematical features of the sub-atomic particles. We form a tight community, seeing one another regularly at conferences and workshops, and often writing papers together where our latest views are displayed. One prominent member of this community is Harald Fritzsch, who became well-known around 1971 when he wrote papers together with Nobel Prize winner Murray Gell-Mann and others, papers in which he laid the roots of a very novel way to understand the behavior of quarks inside protons, pions and other such particles. Quarks were still hypothetical and controversial notions in those days, and his papers showed an expertise that made us believe that the author must have enjoyed a privileged past enabling him to grab one of the many opportunities offered by some top university in the western world.

Few of us, however, were aware at that time that Harald had escaped from Eastern Germany only a few years before, in 1968. He left a a country that was surrounded by a fence or a wall, made practically impenetrable by armed guards and land mines. Life conditions had been harsh there, and students were not allowed even the slightest amount of political freedom to develop and express their own independent views of what an ideal society should be like.

When the local authorities of the town Leipzig, where he studied, decided to bring down a very ancient church in order to create a glorious new Karl Marx Platz, this was just too much for some of the students and other inhabitants to bare, indeed for all those who still cherished some awareness of past culture, other than the modern communist ideals of the time. In this delightful book, the author describes this situation, and what happened next. His protestations had brought him into trouble, and, some way or other, Harald Fritzsch had to leave. He wanted to go to the West anyway, to study quarks and other mysterious riddles that he had read about in the few and scattered scientific renderings that he had been able to put his hands on, and he wanted to work out some very important ideas that he had. Everything, his family, his friends, and his girl friend had to be left behind. He had no choice, and indeed he had to go soon, knowing that the authorities were after him.

This book is of historical importance. It describes the tensions created by a ruthless regime in a defenseless community, the feelings of helplessness as well as the resourcefulness of those who wanted to make a difference, and then had to escape under life threatening conditions. No-one at the time knew whether the tiny pinpricks of the protesters would help at all to bring about any change in a seemingly perpetual situation and whether the monolithic autocrats could maintain their communist rule forever. Indeed, only few could surmise that less than two decades would be needed to bring the cold war to an end. What happened should not be forgotten. Personal accounts such as the one here are real jewels.

Gerard 't Hooft
Institute of Theoretical Physics
Utrecht University
The Netherlands

Prologue

The spotlights were shining across the Sea, back and forth, and then they went out. Maybe we were lucky and they did not spot us. We tried to crouch down as best we could in the little boat, which was filling more and more with water. It looked a little like a submarine gliding on the surface of the water. Only our heads and the motor were visible above the water level. From the viewpoint of the sharp shooters at shore we would not be an easy target due to the waves.

We watched the shore carefully. It was almost dark and we could recognize only a few details of the wooded shoreline. It would have been wiser to stay further out at Sea, away from the sharp shooters on shore; but the waves got higher and we had too much water already in the boat, to take the risk of adding more. Around midnight we reached the bay which we had seen hours before. After the strains of the last hours we were totally exhausted. We recognized a few lights on the horizon, which suggested these must be coming from a village. Having worked our way against the waves for another half hour, we felt we must be close to the shoreline. A sudden noise behind me made me look back, but it was too late. A wall of water came crushing down on us and buried. Because of the darkness, we had not noticed that we were already so close to the beach. The breaker caught us and the boat capsized, throwing us onto the beach.

Extremely exhausted we crawled further onto the shore. After sitting in the boat for such a long time we had to get used to using our limbs again. Our boat was also washed ashore. We pulled it onto the beach with our last remaining strength. Our trip across the Sea had come to an end after about thirty-three hours.

We changed our clothes. Luckily, some of the clothes we had packed inside plastic bags were still dry. Finally, I tried to explore our surroundings. I didn't get far. I heard a voice and I turned around only to look into the light cone of a flashlight. There was a soldier who pointed his gun barrel towards me.

I asked if he spoke Russian: "Goworite pa russki?" An unintelligible sentence followed. The soldier pulled the rifle up making me raise both my hands instinctively.

Contents

Autumn 1967

In the winter term of 1963 I began my studies in physics and mathematics at the University of Leipzig, I was twenty years old. Between my German High School graduation at the Gerhart-Hauptmann High School in Zwickau and the beginning of my time as a university student, I was a radio operator in the Air Force of the army. I was based in the school for pilots in the city of Kamenz near Dresden.

But the story of this book started later, in the autumn of 1967. At that time I was sick with flu and therefore could not take part in the practical work which was required for all students.

In those days all students had to spend two weeks in October helping farmers with their potato harvest. I cannot say that I was overly enthusiastic about traveling to Mecklenburg for this purpose; but those weeks fostered a closer sense of community among the students. Lifelong friendships began in those potato fields, sometimes even leading to marriages, although the campsites had not been exactly comfortable quarters.

Since my illness had not permitted me to go to the fields, I was sent by the FDJ (Federal Communist Youth) organization to the Physics Institute at Leipzig University, to do some practical work in the library. When I showed up at the library administration office, I was told, to my astonishment, that I was to go to the University Church the following day. It turned out that part of the library stocks was stored in the side wings of that church.

St Paul's University Church was called by most people Paulinerkirche; it was located on Karl-Marx Square, north of the Augusteum, the main building of the university. This was the only university church in Saxony that was not destroyed. The church even survived the Anglo-American air raid offensive on December 4, 1943 during World War II. Since the roofs were built on a steep slope, the bombs were diverted to neighboring buildings and did not damage the interior of the church. Thanks to the courageous efforts of the people of Leipzig, the church also escaped the fires which destroyed a major part of the city.

Inside St Paul's Church there was still a part of the cloisters of the Dominican Abbey, founded in 1229; at that time it was located directly inside the eastern city wall. This Abbey was dedicated in 1240, and renovated in the fifteenth century. Martin Luther changed it into a Protestant church in 1545. It has been used as the university auditorium ever since the year 1545.

In old travel guide books of Leipzig you would read: "St Paul's Church was known as one of the most splendid, well-preserved open churches of Middle Germany. It was ornate with tombs, epitaphs and other artifacts, intertwined with a tradition of Johann Sebastian Bach's music and the history of the reformation." As ordered by the Government of the DDR (Democratic Republic of Germany), travel books on Leipzig published in East Germany after 1968 did not give any references to the university church.

On the first day of my assignment to this building on Karl-Marx Square, I made my way there on a bicycle. After I rang the door bell several times, a small side door was opened by Mrs Werner, an elderly employee of the university library. She led me to a spiral staircase which we climbed to reach "her domain" — a fairly remarkable library consisting of mostly old, dust-covered volumes.

"My God" said Mrs Werner, "they sent you here? I would love to know who thought of this nonsense. I have no work for you. I have to take inventory of the books myself anyway."

"Well," I told her, "I better go back to the main office, maybe they'll send me somewhere else."

"Don't do that. You know what, why don't you just stay here and keep me company. I'll get you a desk and you can bring your books tomorrow and work here. This is more convenient than the German Library. At the end of your time here, I'll sign the form telling the administration that you worked for two weeks, which is actually even true."

"Perfect, that's done!" I grinned. "I'll be here tomorrow morning with my books."

The following days at the university library were pleasant. Mrs Werner left me to do my own things without disturbing me. The only condition was that I would drink coffee with her often. I gladly did that since her coffee was excellent — almost as good as the one from my landlady in Leipzig. At times I rummaged through the old books and read Shakespeare in the original language, or Dante, and even Galileo's *Discorsi* was there.

The library also housed history books about the university — the old Universitas Litterarum Lipsiensis, which had been founded in 1409, making it the fourth oldest university of all of the German-speaking universities of that time. In the meantime, its name had been changed to Karl-Marx University in 1953, the year of the national uprising against the regime of the SED (Sozialistische Einheitspartei Deutschlands, the former East German Party of Socialist Unity). The name change had been suggested by Chairman Ulbricht of the DDR government and it prevailed in the Party Center. There were lots of name changes, equally absurd, for example the city of Chemnitz turned into Karl-Marx City. Karl-Marx had never been in Leipzig, nor had he had any affiliation with the university. He received his doctorate at the University of Jena — without ever having studied there.

The square where the church was located, had been called Augustus Square, named after King Friedrich August of Saxony, and had been renamed Karl-Marx Square. The older people of Leipzig, like Mrs Werner and my landlady, simply ignored the new name and continued to speak of the Augustus Square. One day, during a coffee break, Mrs Werner said mockingly, calling Chairman Ulbricht "goatee", his nickname among the people, that the "goatee" might even have the idea of changing the name of University Church to Karl-Marx Church. She had no idea that the party leader had an even more sinister plan of what to do with the church.

Mrs Werner was an expert in the history of this university. She told me that between 1835 and 1873 the Augusteum housed the Physics Institute. The Augusteum was a beautiful classicistic building, which was completed in 1835. The entrance door was designed by the famous German architect and painter Karl Friedrich Schinkel. The main wing of the building was destroyed during World War II, with the exception of the church's front and the long side wings. They housed individual institutes, libraries, and lecture halls.

Mrs Werner spoke enthusiastically about the Lecture Hall 40 of the Augusteum, which was, for a while, the intellectual center of East Germany. The lectures of Professor Hans Mayer in this auditorium were legendary; and the same held for those of the philosopher Ernst Bloch.

"Just imagine, Mr Fritzsch, what Bloch said one day when speaking about Immanuel Kant: 'Immanuel Kant was born, lived and died in Kaliningrad.'" We had to laugh so hard. Shortly after Bloch's description of Kant, he received an express letter from Paul Froehlich, the party chief of the SED in Leipzig, in which he expressed that Bloch was no longer welcome at the Institute. Bloch left for Tuebingen. "What a country we live in."

I also learned from Mrs Werner that until the 1930s, many great physics lectures were held at the Augusteum. Werner Heisenberg, already world famous in his early years, received a chair in Theoretical Physics in 1927. Another Augusteum lecturer was Ludwig Boltzmann, the founder of the theory of modern atomic and thermodynamic theory, who had come to Leipzig in 1900.

In the fall of 1967, I started working on my doctoral thesis. The director of the Theoretical Physics Institute, Gerhard Heber had suggested that I go for my PhD without going through a time-consuming detour of a Master's thesis. My dissertation dealt with problems of gravitational theory, which interested me particularly. Professor Hans-Juergen Treder, the director of the department of theoretical physics of the Academy of Science in Berlin, had already shown interest in my project. So I worked under his guidance. Treder worked in the observatory in Potsdam-Babelsberg. Starting with the winter term of 1967, I was a PhD student, shuttling back and forth between Leipzig and Potsdam. I rented a room in a nice street in the old part of Potsdam.

While still completing my work in St Paul's Church, I read a new book by Werner Heisenberg, who was, at that time, director of the Max-Planck Institute of Physics in Munich. In his book, Heisenberg describes his ideas of a unified theory of elementary particles and therefore, of all of matter. His special interest was in the area of strong interaction between atomic nuclei. Experimentally, it had been shown, for quite some time, that very strong attractive forces act between the nucleons, the protons and neutrons inside the atomic nuclei. The origin of these forces was completely unknown at that time.

Heisenberg believed that these forces could be described with the help of a simple mathematical equation. This equation was dubbed "world formula", not by Heisenberg himself, but by the press, a highly exaggerated name as it turned out to be. I had my doubts about Heisenberg's approach to the phenomenon of nuclear forces — after all, I had, for some time, occupied myself with the writings of Murray Gell-Mann of the California Institute of

Technology in Pasadena. In his papers, Gell-Mann defended his ideas that much smaller particles exist within the atoms; particles which he had called quarks. (The name is derived from James Joyce's book *Finnegan's Wake*).

Although I initially had a hard time believing that atomic nuclei were composed of particles smaller than the nuclear particles themselves, Gell-Mann's arguments convinced me. His daring hypothesis would be able to explain a series of experimentally proven phenomena — amongst them some odd symmetry patterns of elementary particles. Only one thing remained inexplicable: the question of the forces between quarks. These forces had to be extremely strong, much stronger than the forces between nuclei. This implied that the nuclear forces were nothing but what remained after the very strong forces between the quarks had acted inside the atomic nuclear particles.

During the summer vacation in 1967, I had worked on this problem without gaining new insights other than those that I found in the papers of Gell-Mann. In Heisenberg's book I found a hint for a new way of approaching the question of how to describe the forces between elementary particles. This had first been approached by two American theoretical physicists: C.N. Yang and S. Mills. One day I surprised Mrs Werner when I arrived on my bike with a big batch of books, including a thick volume of the American journal *Physical Review*.

"Oh my God, Mr Fritzsch, what are you doing with all those books, as though I didn't have enough of them?"

"Unfortunately, they are not the right ones for me, but don't worry, I won't read all of them. I am looking for something specific."

In the following days I read everything I could find about the Yang–Mills theory at the library of the Physics Institute and at the German Library. Unfortunately I did not find much about this topic. In an article by the Nobel laureate Richard Feynman, a colleague of Gell-Mann's in Pasadena, I read that the Yang–Mills theory is very useful for studying these unsolved problems that combine quantum physics with the theory of gravity. Indeed, there are parallels between the ideas of Yang and Mills and the theory of gravity, which Einstein had created in 1915.

I now tried to apply the ideas of Yang and Mills to the forces between quarks. During my stay at St Paul's Church I examined a series of alternatives, but stopped there since I saw no possibility of clearly differentiating the various versions. I would need new experimental insights to get ahead.

At that time I could not foresee that three years later, after my escape from the DDR, I would start at the same point that I had reached in October 1967, but this time at Stanford University in California. In the summer of 1970, I got to know Murray Gell-Mann, who received the Nobel Prize in Physics in 1969 for his contributions to particle physics, at the Aspen Center of Physics in Colorado. Our common interests in physics brought us together. We became friends, and for several years we worked together, both at the California Institute of Technology in Pasadena, and also at the European Center of Elementary Particle Physics (CERN) in Geneva, Switzerland.

Shortly before I left California in the spring of 1971, I told Gell-Mann of my studies in Leipzig in trying to describe the forces between quarks using elements of the Yang–Mills theory. Although he was initially skeptical, my remarks seemed to get him interested. When we met again in the autumn of 1971 to work at CERN for a year, we continued to work along these lines. But it was not until the summer of 1972 before we were able to find the key to understand the forces between quarks. Indeed, they proved to be forces that can be described by a Yang-Mills type theory. The forces are due to force particles which we called gluons.

In hindsight, my studies in Leipzig were quite useful. The theory itself, which we later called "Quantum Chromodynamics", proved to be the correct theoretical description of the forces between quarks, and also of the strong forces inside atomic nuclei. This is an important building block of today's physics. To me, it will always remind me of St Paul's Church in Leipzig.

Rheinsberg

Back in mid-October in 1967, the university became alive again. The students returned from their work in Mecklenburg. I was looking forward to the return of one particular medical student, Susanne Kocian. I had met her two years ago at the German Library where she was preparing for an early examination.

Since I lived close to the library, I made a habit of spending a fair amount of time in its reading room. I studied physics and mathematics monographs and solved exercises. But I also read a lot of books on philosophy, history and literature.

One day I spotted the extremely attractive young woman there. When I saw her again the following day, I made sure to sit close to her. A volume of Bertrand Russell next to all the physics books made her look up and we began a conversation which lasted until late that evening.

Susanne was from the southern part of East Germany — just as I was — from the region of Annaberg in the Erzgebirge Mountains. Her father was from Prague in Czechoslovakia and had married her mother in Dresden during the war. He had died there in the early 1950s from the aftermath of severe war injuries. Her mother then moved back to her hometown where she had a successful medical practice.

We quickly became good friends since we shared many interests and hobbies like going to concerts, theater and reading literature. We also took many bicycle and motorcycle rides.

Susanne rented a room from Mrs Elsheimer on Stoetteritz Street, not far from my place at 26 Holstein Street, in the east of Leipzig. On my first visit to Susanne, I met Mrs Elsheimer and realized that she knew my landlady, Mrs Hempel. Both were over sixty years old. My landlady was well-known in that part of the city, because her husband Wilhelm Hempel — whom she married as a young girl during World War I — had been the captain of the German National Soccer team. He died shortly before the end of the war.

Mrs Hempel never married again. She always rented out two rooms to students. She looked after these students as though they were her own children. She was a wonderful landlady, maybe one of the last of her kind, which may not exist anymore. But she stuck to one rule for her renters: no lady visitors after ten in the evening, without exception.

Mrs Elsheimer was not as strict. Susanne arranged, from time to time, that we would enjoy Mrs Hempel's excellent cooking and then had coffee at Mrs Elsheimer's.

Both Susanne and I had learned to work fast, but intensively, which gave us ample free time to be together. During the summer we would go swimming in the Canal near Burghausen. On one of those excursions, Susanne read to me "Rheinsberg", a lovely story by Kurt Tucholsky. I had read this story before, but never had I experienced it as I did at that time. Ever since, we called the little hill "our Rheinsberg", and I am sure Tucholsky would have approved, even though there was no castle as in the story.

We enjoyed the extensive musical activities of the town. The concerts given by the Gewandhaus Orchestra or the Radio Orchestra were mostly at the large Congress Hall. This hall would play a special part in my life in the summer of 1968.

A short time after the first performance of every new program, we would visit the political cabaret called "Die Pfeffermuehle" (pepper mill) located next to St Thomas Church. The first performance always happened during the "Leipzig Messe", and nobody knew how long it would be before this program would be forbidden to remain open. One day, after the "Leipzig Messe", a performer of "Die Pfeffermuehle" announced: "Yesterday we were closed, today we are open, but if we are too big-mouthed, we will be closed again tomorrow!" Sure enough, the next day, it was closed.

As far as the material needs of my life were concerned, I was better off than most students. As a former soldier, I received a scholarship and also help from my parents. I had access to about as much money as a construction worker would earn. My comfortable room cost me little, and there was no tuition fee. So, I had a relatively comfortable existence.

In the spring of 1967, I asked Susanne to join me in the following summer on a trip with my folding canoe. I planned to go from Krakow or Warsaw on the river Weichsel to the mouth of the river at Danzig. But Susanne was unable to join me since she had to do an internship at the clinic. So a friend and colleague of mine, Lothar Hill, joined me instead. What I learned on this trip was going to be decisive for my later escape across the Black Sea.

In the Bay of Danzig — Summer of 1967

I had known Lothar Hill since my military service as a radio operator in the Air Force in Kamenz. We had met in 1962 when Lothar had to quit pilot training at the flight school for political reasons. One day he showed up at my unit. We talked often about physics, which he also wanted to study, as well as philosophy, and later on, politics.

He had joined the army as a committed communist with the goal of becoming an officer and a MiG fighter pilot. But the constant political indoctrination produced the opposite effect. He thought about things more carefully than most others; and as a result, doubts about the prevailing Marxist–Leninist doctrines crept into his thoughts. When he began to openly express his doubts in class, he was coaxed — in vain — to think in a politically correct way. He then asked to be relieved from the flight school, so that he could serve the remainder of his military service as an ordinary soldier. His superior officers granted his wish after intense discussions.

Slowly, our conversations took on a risky character. Both of us recognized the hollowness of the prevailing state ideology, and we talked about it freely, which was not without danger. Although we were careful not to be overheard, we could never be sure of that within the military premises.

We arranged so that we were often jointly assigned to guard the planes. This made it possible for us to sit down in a corner to listen at night to a little battery operated radio, tuned to BBC (British Broadcasting Corporation) and RIAS (Rundfunk im amerikanischen Sektor), a free radio station in West Berlin. Needless to say, it was strictly forbidden to listen to any Western radio station. Any violation would lead to severe punishment.

During the first winter of my military service, I was assigned several times to perform guard duty at the entrance gate of the Kamenz flight school. I spent my time listening to the radio with tiny headphones which could not be detected under the steel helmet we had to wear. One day while listening to the news on the RIAS station, the commander of the air force, General Kessler, came to visit our unit. His Soviet luxury limousine suddenly stopped at the gate and I had not enough time to take my ear phones out and turn off the radio. I had to give the usual report while the newscast was ringing in my ears. General Kessler, who was in a good mood that day, got out of the car and began to talk to me about everyday problems of the barracks. I was lucky he did not realize that I had a hard time understanding him. I do not want to think what could have happened had he found out the reason of my poor hearing on that occasion.

One night, when Lothar and I again had guard duty, we met at a corner of the airfield. The planes, which were old Soviet propeller aircrafts, were clearly visible in the moonlight. We leaned our Kalaschnikov submachine guns against the crate we sat on, and finally, I had the opportunity to ask Lothar a long overdue question: "The border with Bavaria is 200 kilometers away from Kamenz. Do you think we could make it to Bavaria if we secretly prepared one of these planes for take-off?" Lothar looked at me astonished. "Are you aware how dangerous that is? If we get caught, then God help us. It means fifteen years jail in the military prison Bautzen II."

"I am aware of that, but once we sit in an airplane, who could keep us from fleeing? I don't see any reason that you with your pilot's license couldn't fly a plane to Bavaria. That would be one opportunity for us to escape to the West, which wouldn't come again soon."

"Let us talk about this again in a few days. In the meantime I'll get some information from the flight school."

With that, we ended our secret meeting. Just in time, since I saw a figure sneaking around the planes. This was, I assumed, a routine check by the control officer of the guards. I pulled up my machine gun and in accordance with our rules, called out, "Stop! Who is there?"

The officer answered and everything seemed to be okay. He continued walking to the other corner of the airfield and a few minutes later, I could hear Lothar calling out, "Stop! Who is there?"

I breathed a sigh of relief. The week before, the guard control officer caught me sleeping on the wing of a plane. Two days detention was the consequence, which I did not mind too much. I used the time to work on problems of physics.

A week later, Lothar and I had another chance to discuss our escape plans. Lothar had, in the meantime, spoken to a friend of the MiG fighter flight school. This friend told him in detail about the security of the air space of East Germany. There was no way for us to carry out an escape by plane. A slow propeller aircraft, like ours, would inevitably show up on the radar screen of the Soviet MiG fighter interceptor, which constantly patrolled the Western borders, about half an hour before anybody could reach the border. It would be a miracle not to be hit by the anti-aircraft missiles. That was enough for us to shelve our plans for the time being.

In the summer of 1962, shortly before the Cuba Crisis which brought the world close to an atomic war, our unit was sent to a summer camp in the Erzgebirge Mountains close to Annaberg. From there to the Bavarian border it was only 80 kilometers. That meant it was only a 25-minute flight.

After only a few days at the camp I considered again the possibility of escaping by night with one of the planes. I believed we would have a good chance of succeeding since we could fly low through the valleys of this mountain range. But it meant that Lothar, who had stayed in Kamenz, had to specially come to the Erzgebirge Mountains. But due to the tense political situation, it was impossible to take leave from one's unit, except in special circumstances. I finally abandoned my escape plan and decided to finish my studies in Leipzig first.

Today, when I think back to the time of my stay in the National People's Army, I realize that quite a few of my comrades were thinking of escaping to the West. In this context, the wildest plans were contemplated. I remember that at the time our unit was in Mecklenburg during the fall harvest, I met two soldiers of an armored division stationed close to the Potsdam border. We seriously discussed the possibility of taking an armored vehicle to break through the border to West Berlin. But this border action during the tense political time would lead to a long gun battle with uncertain ending.

Lothar and I tried to calculate how to construct a helium balloon which we could use, under favorable wind conditions, to escape to the West. But we soon gave up that idea because we were unable to get the necessary materials and the required amount of helium (or a substitute gas). We continued to make plans, which remained in the planning stages. None of them got into the hands of the STASI (*Ministerium für Staatsicherheit*, the East Germany secret police agency) informants, or were overheard by them.

After being discharged by the army in the spring of 1963, I stayed for a few months with my parents in Reinsdorf near Zwickau. My classes at Leipzig University did not start until the fall. I could not decide, at that time, whether to study physics or mathematics, so I studied both at the same time. A decision I delayed for five semesters, after which I made my final decision to study physics only. I realized that my interests were geared towards natural phenomena and less towards the artificial structures of mathematics.

I met Lothar Hill again at the university. We ended up in the same study group. During the semester break we took a few trips together, among them a trip to Poland in the summer of 1967.

I owned a folding canoe which could be easily packed into two bags. At the end of July we took a train to Warsaw and stayed for two days at the camping grounds along the river Weichsel. We did some sightseeing in the Polish capitol. Then we started our journey paddling in the direction of Danzig. On the first day we met a very tall Polish man from Krakow, who also wanted to go to Danzig by canoe. So we joined him. Our companion's name was Stefan Popovich; he was a lecturer of engineering at Krakow University. He made the trip alone because his girlfriend did not show up.

Stefan told us that he had taken this long trip down the river from Krakow to Danzig every year for the last decade accompanied by a series of female students. None of them lasted the whole trip; most of them quit before they reached Warsaw. But he had made up his mind that he would get married only if he found a woman who was capable of holding on for the full journey.

In the evenings we built a large campfire next to the river and Stefan told us a lot about Poland and about everyday life at the university. During one of those evenings, we talked about the Baltic Sea shore and he mentioned that in the Bay of Danzig one was allowed to take a small boat out to the open sea. Lothar and I were skeptical since this would be unthinkable on the shores of Eastern Germany. We decided to look into this point once we got to Danzig.

It took us ten days to arrive there. The exit from the bay to the ocean was not permitted in a small boat like ours for safety reasons. So, we had to take a tributary of the river to the Danzig port. At that point, the border police became aware of our boat. A fast police boat stopped us. After looking at out papers they told us that we could not continue paddling parallel to the beach. We wanted to reach the sea port Sobot north of Danzig and stay there on the camping grounds. We grumbled and had no other choice but to fold our boat together and take the bus to Sobot.

We stayed right there for almost a week. The campsite was south of the city not far from a beautiful sandy beach, where we assembled our boat. I wanted to find out if our small folding canoe was stable enough for the sea. Such an experiment was only possible outside the GDR. In East Germany it was not even permitted to use an inflatable rubber boat at the beaches. Any violation resulted in imprisonment since it was always viewed as an attempt to flee the country.

I told Lothar a story that I had heard in Leipzig shortly before we left there. Last summer a student tried to escape in a folding canoe from the Darss Peninsula, which was a heavily overgrown nature reserve, to Denmark. During the night he assembled his boat, but when he wanted to take it into the water he was stopped by the border patrol. To the question what he was doing, he answered that he was taking a walk.

"What about the boat? Don't you know that it is forbidden to bring any boat to the beach?" The student answered that he did not want to use it; he just wanted to go on a walk with the boat. "This is a hobby of mine and surely not forbidden." The judge later on thought that this was a brazen answer he gave to the border patrol. So he gave him three additional months in jail on top of the usual fine for attempting to escape the country.

At about the same time, I had taken a trip with Susanne to the Baltic Sea in order to take this opportunity to study the shoreline at Darss. The idea to attempt an escape from there was dropped pretty soon after I saw the extensive border protection.

Lothar and I trained daily with the boat, even in the choppy seas, and in doing so, made a noteworthy discovery. Even with waves of about one meter height, we could handle the boat as long as the waves did not fold over. Our folding canoe was six meters long and was able to adjust to the shape of the waves; with careful navigation, there was almost no real danger of capsizing.

This experience in practice confirmed the theoretical knowledge about folding canoes at high sea, which I had carefully looked into at the German Library. The librarian must have been astonished that, next to all the physics books, I took out books on folding canoes. I read with great interest about the first Atlantic crossing with a canoe in the 1920s. At least I learned that these canoes were much more adaptable on the high sea than most people thought.

Once, we went far out on the Danzig Bay until a patrol boat, located out there, came towards us with flashing signals. They ordered us to turn around immediately and go back to shore. While paddling back to shore I said to Lothar, "If those patrol boats were not here we could keep paddling out to the open sea all the way to Sweden."

Lothar's answer was short enough, "Yes, if."

"Let's assume we tried it at night. They wouldn't see us. We could maneuver between those boats without being noticed, and then go on to Sweden. Our boat is so small, has no metallic material, so it would not be visible by radar."

"You wouldn't see anything on the radar screen, but on the infrared detectors … "

I had not thought about that. Lothar was correct. As a former officer's candidate he was well aware of the tricks of the border patrol. I had also heard about the infrared devices that kept the entire coastline of the Baltic Sea in the GDR under surveillance. Anything on water and that is warmer than water could be detected, like a swimmer, even at night. Two men in a canoe would be immediately detected.

"Do you think there are infrared detectors all along the shoreline of the Eastern countries?" I asked Lothar.

"Most certainly here along the Baltic Sea shore. Let's put it this way: I doubt that the Russians have detectors along the endless coastlines of Siberia. I guess they are not needed there. Or do you want to take a folding canoe to Vladivostock?"

"No, but I am thinking of the Black Sea. I have heard that you can take a boat, even a larger boat, and go out to sea without any problem in Rumania and in the north of Bulgaria. This is not allowed in the south of Bulgaria or in East Germany. Maybe there are no infrared detectors in the north of Bulgaria because nobody thinks anyone is crazy enough to go to Turkey in a 'nutshell'."

"You know what? If that is correct, that would be an interesting discovery."

"No hypothesis. It was just a thought. But it would be a good thing to take a look at the Black Sea."

Lothar and I discussed our future on that evening at a campfire. We had not really spoken about concrete plans for escape from East Germany since the time of our military service. I had avoided the topic with friends at the university, except in the most abstract and speculative way. The reason is clear. Even the smallest hint of suspicion of planning an escape could lead to an arrest or at least an interrogation by the Secret Police (STASI). We knew that there was an informant in every student group.

After all, I had, for a long time, been planning to get away from East Germany on completion of my studies. Ever since I was twelve years old I had decided to study physics and mathematics in order to work on fundamental research. Since my parents were of the middle class — my father was a building contractor and kept his company afloat in spite of all the difficulties with the bureaucracy of the planning department — there was only one way to make a career in research in this system, and that was to join the Communist Youth Group and later the SED (East Germany Communist Party). I certainly did not want to do this.

An important factor in my decision to leave the country, made before I was fourteen years old, was the constant discrimination against children of businessmen, freelance doctors, or children of self-employed people. When one of the teachers asked me what kind of future I saw for myself, I answered that I intended to study to become a physicist or mathematician. He laughed and said, "Then you should have chosen another father. Only children of workers and farmers go on to study here, in our society — write that behind your ears."

The teacher who, by and large, was a nice and genial man, did not want to be mean, but he had simply reflected the prevailing attitudes, and that was a shock to me. From that point on, I paid more attention to political matters; and I also made a point to listen surreptitiously to Western radio stations. When the Soviet Army suppressed the Hungarian uprising in 1956, I was certain that I would leave East Germany after finishing high school.

In the summer of 1961, when I was eighteen years old, shortly after receiving my high school diploma in Zwickau, I went by bicycle to the border of East Germany close to the town of Plauen. This trip, which was taken a short time after the borders in East Germany were closed and a brick wall had been erected all around the city of East Berlin, was meant to be an exploratory trip to show me more what that border was like. After all, I had already planned to flee from that location before I would have to start my military service in the army, which was to begin in October.

Unfortunately, I was caught by the border patrol just inside the five-kilometer wide border zone, and was brought to a frontier station. For the first time in my life — and I might add, the only time — I found myself in a jail cell. I was held for several hours and finally interrogated. Obviously, I denied having any plans to flee and showed them my draft papers for the army and my student pass of the University of Leipzig. They were impressed, and in the evening I was brought by two officers to Plauen where they put me on the train to Zwickau.

This excursion, which ended quite luckily for me, taught me that trying to cross the border from East Germany to West Germany was much more difficult than I had imagined. So, I decided to finish my military service and my studies, and then escape to the West after my examination.

Today, I realize that my early decision to leave East Germany made a big difference in my further development. I was, so to speak, an East German citizen "on call". Therefore, I could think about my career free of any constraint of the system. During political discussions at the university, I often spoke my mind freely, but without being provocative.

But foremost, I wanted to finish my studies quickly. The top brass of the Communist Youth Group and of the SED party thought that I was a student with different ideas, but that I was not completely lost to them. There were several attempts to get me to be more politically correct and active. But those attempts were in vain.

During the semester break I explored different escape possibilities, sometimes by myself, and sometimes with friends. Lothar and I went on a motorcycle trip through the Boehmerwald (Bohemian Forest) along the Czech border towards Austria and West Germany in order to get to know the area better. Extensive hikes through the woods permitted us to form a clear picture about the border security, which turned out not to be in our favor. We were once stopped by a Czech border patrol close to the Austrian border and interrogated for several hours. After our particulars were taken down, we were set free again — there was no proof of any wrong doing.

During several weeks studying in Leningrad, I had taken extensive trips to the North in order to explore the possibilities of escaping via Karelia to Finland. After talking to local farmers, I soon learned enough that it was almost impossible getting across the border zone which was some 50 kilometers wide. Even the locals would have a hard time crossing this area without being noticed. But should the crossing of the zone be successful, getting across the actual border would have been truly dangerous.

Much later, at the end of the 1970s, I met a Jewish physicist at Harvard University, who had indeed crossed the border from the Soviet Union to Finland, and we exchanged experiences. It took him several weeks to get across. He had traveled only by night, and had advanced slowly to the border without being detected. His only nourishment had been the berries and mushrooms that he found on his journey.

Back to our exploration in Poland: on that particular evening at the Sobot beach, I openly spoke to Lothar about fleeing East Germany. Lothar answered with reservations. It turned out that he had convinced himself of the possibility that true socialism could be attained. He pointed out the rising democratization of political life in the Czech Republic. In Poland things were also in motion: during our trip we had noticed how people there were much freer and less constrained than in East Germany.

I remained skeptical and did not foresee any chance of a new beginning in Eastern Europe at that time. The countries depended too much on the Soviet Union, and there was no sign of reform over there.

"Let's wait and see what is going to happen in Prague until next summer," answered Lothar. "We can always escape later. I found it extremely interesting what you said earlier about the Black Sea. We should have a look at it, maybe next semester."

The following day we folded our boat together and took the train back to Leipzig.

As a Scout in Bulgaria — November 1967

At the beginning of the winter term in 1967, Lothar and I had already pinned down the exact date of our planned trip to Bulgaria. Being fairly advanced in our studies, we needed only to attend a few more lectures and practical training sessions, and that was not a problem. We decided to travel in the second half of November. We told none of our friends about our plans.

A Bulgarian friend provided us with a private invitation to Sofia; that was needed in order to get a visa for this trip. As I said before, we started towards the end of the second week in November. We took the train and arrived two days later at Bucharest, the capital of Rumania, via Prague and Budapest. This was our first planned stop of our journey.

When we arrived that morning, we first took care of our lodgings, and then we went to the West German embassy, which was located in the outskirts of the city. There we wanted to inform ourselves about the border security along the Rumanian Black Sea coast. But when we approached the embassy, we realized that that was impossible. The villa, which housed the embassy, was surrounded by police, and all visitors had to identify themselves. Lothar and I were disappointed, turned back and consoled ourselves with a really good meal in a restaurant in the center of the city.

The next day, we continued our journey and arrived on the same day at the Bulgarian capital Sofia, the destination of our trip.

We stayed at the apartment of a friend, Boris Slavov, whom we knew from Leipzig. He had studied physics in Leipzig.

The next few days, we went sightseeing with Boris all over the city and visited the nearby Witoscha Mountain Range. On another day, we went to the West German embassy in Sofia, which was also surrounded by police. But Boris had told us that visitors to the embassy did not have to identify themselves to the police.

When the doorman heard that we came from East Germany, he went inside to get an embassy employee who guided us in the right direction. After a few hints on our part, he realized that our trip and our visit to the embassy was motivated by our attempt to escape, and motioned us to be quiet. We followed him without a word to the second floor and into a large room which included a small windowless cubbyhole.

"Now, here we can talk," he said. "I'm sorry to put you in this cubbyhole, but we had to install it. It is acoustically and electronically isolated. Two years ago the Bulgarian Secret Service installed itself across the street, and ever since, we are being monitored with special devices. So, what is it you want?"

We told him that we wanted to know the details of the border security along the Black Sea coast, in particular, about infrared devices. We realized quickly that the man had no idea what infrared systems were; maybe he simply did not want us to be aware of what he did know. In any case, it became apparent to us that we could not get any useful information from him.

We kept on chatting with this embassy employee for a while, and he appeared to be interested in knowing our travel plans. He warned us against attempting to flee over any land route into Yugoslavia or Turkey. The Bulgarian border patrol was feared even more than that of East Germany. It was a matter of course for them to use their rifles, and to them, human life counted for very little.

Finally, we started back to the apartment but not without making sure that nobody followed us. The following day, we began the second part of our trip. Boris accompanied us to the train station. The train brought us in a few hours to Varna, which is a seaport in the north of the country.

Northeast of Varna there is the old vacation spot called Druzba. A little further was "Zlatni Pjasaci" — the "Golden Sand" — a long stretch of beach which was then easily accessible. Today, it is covered with hotels. A taxi driver took us to Druzba; he spoke little German and suggested a nice hotel that was directly by the beach. This was November and the hotels were almost empty, so we got a nice large room with a balcony looking out on the beach.

It was already late afternoon, the sun set slowly, and we began our work. We used binoculars, a Zeiss product with a considerable zooming capability. Lothar and I took turns to watch out for boats on the horizon. We observed that a row of small boats appeared at dusk. They were positioned at about two kilometers from the next one and appeared to be stationary. The grouping of the boats reminded me of the chain of boats I had noticed off the coast at Darss and of Ruegen on the Baltic Sea. Only the distance between the boats was now larger, which was a comforting sign. We marked the position of the ships on a piece of paper and then went to dinner at the hotel restaurant.

After dinner, we took a walk along the beach. I tried to make a mental imprint of the location of the hotels, and also of the nearby camping site that we had discovered before. Around nine o'clock we were back in our hotel room and we continued to observe the sea. As we had expected, the boats were nearly at the same position as before. Without a doubt, these were border patrol boats.

We also followed the motion of the boats coming from the port of Varna. Larger and smaller ships came and went. In short, we saw nothing exciting, so we went to bed.

The rising sun awakened me the next morning. I realized that Lothar was up already, standing on the balcony. "It's about time that you got up. I have already done the first shift of guard duty." "How is it going with the boats?" I asked drowsily. "Are they still out there?" "No sign of them. I had awakened shortly before sunrise and immediately tried to observe them, but they were gone. I take it they left way before daybreak." "Excellent, it probably means that during the day nobody makes a point of observing movement on the waters. Not bad, in any case, it looks more favorable than on the Baltic Sea. I have to say that the Black Sea is growing on me."

After breakfast we walked in a northerly direction with the intention to learn more details about the border security. We left the hotels behind us and walked along the beach. Beyond the bay we saw the houses of the next village called Balcik, a small fishing town. While looking through the binoculars, I remember seeing a large radar installation on a hill. Clearly, its job was the surveillance of passing ships out there in the Black Sea.

"There you have it," said Lothar. "With this installation they want to recognize boats that might try to leave during the night."

"You can't see a folding canoe with that," I answered. "Even a boat with a small outboard motor would not be noticed with this radar. There are no infrared installations anywhere around here."

"I doubt that there are infrared installations in this region of the coast, maybe they have them only on their patrol boats. But even there I have my doubts. Basically, that makes sense. If you want to flee to Turkey from here, you need a bigger boat since it is more than 200 kilometers to Turkey. The idea that a small folding canoe would try to go all the way to Turkey, I'm sure nobody finds this reasonable. It would be an insane venture."

I recounted a story I had been told by friends in Zwickau. Twin brothers, sons of a medical doctor from the Erzgebirge Mountains, tried to flee in a rubber boat from a Bulgarian town south of Ahtopol, located near the Turkish border. The border patrol discovered their boat with infrared devices just before the boat crossed the border line. They fired grenades at the boat, killing both brothers.

It was no use trying to flee from a town in Southern Bulgaria. There might be a chance in the north. The border installations had to be circumvented way out at sea. The region of Varna, way up in the north, seemed to be a good starting point of departure for an escape.

The following two days that we remained in Varna were used for scouting the closer proximity of the town. We tried to get in contact with people there, speaking Russian as well as we could, in order to learn more about security along the coast. All information led to the same conclusion that we had: the Bulgarian border defense relied on radar surveillance in the north, and the mesh of patrol boats during the night.

Those were positive news. In an optimistic mood, we left Varna. Two days later we were back in Leipzig.

Spring in Prague

I spent some of the last weeks of 1967 in Potsdam in order to get ahead with my studies at the Stellar Observatory at Potsdam–Babelsberg with Professor Treder. In February, at the end of the winter term of 1968, I went to stay with my parents for a few weeks. There I did my initial work towards writing my PhD thesis. I made great strides and by the beginning of the summer term in April, I had finished the first part. That was good because in the following eventful weeks I had little time to concentrate on physics.

Spring in Prague was in full swing. At the university we constantly discussed the events in Czechoslovakia. Alexander Dubcek, the Slovakian party leader and reformer, was our hero. For us and many other students in East Germany, the new direction there was interesting because it seemed to be an alternative to the western bourgeois social system, whose values were, for many of us, too one-sidedly tied to private property. Finally, we had a perspective for our own country. Although, I had planned for years to leave East Germany, I now became hesitant. Why should I leave if there was a chance for a change?

In the beginning of April 1968, Susanne and I traveled to Prague in order to see for ourselves the new developments. The impression was overwhelming. We heard, for the first time, from students and lecturers of the University of Prague what it meant to be free, and to think and speak freely and independently. But what impressed me most were the enormous optimism and the unfailing self-assurance with which the reformers worked in spite of the warnings from Moscow and the capitals of the other East European countries. Half a year later, the whole world knew that this optimism was not justified.

We were so impressed with the changes in Prague that we began to think seriously of similar reforms in East Germany. Together with friends we often discussed through the night the possibility of starting a reform movement in East Germany. Sometimes we started the conversations in the university cafeteria, where we always had to reckon with informants of the STASI being among us.

The city of Leipzig seemed to be a good starting point for a reform movement — better than East Berlin, since the government at the capital was too much under the control of the party leadership of the SED and of the state security services. In addition, Leipzig was also much more cosmopolitan than the capital; after all, twice a year there were fairs in Leipzig which attracted many visitors from Western countries.

In our discussions, the outlines for the reforms played a major role. Robert Havemann, professor of physical chemistry at Humboldt University in East Berlin, had, for years, discussed reforms in his legendary lectures and talks. I studied with great care Havemann's writings. Although I could not follow all the ideas he put forward, especially his unrealistic economic political ideas, he was nonetheless our idol. He was the example we wanted to emulate. Unfortunately, he did not live to reap the harvest of his thoughts, which he had already formulated in the 1960s and which became a reality in the peaceful revolution of East Germany in the fall of 1989. He had been harassed and kept in isolation by the communist regime for decades; he died in 1982.

At the end of April, Lothar and I decided to travel to Prague to celebrate May Day with the reformers. At that time, it was almost the duty of students to participate in demonstrations on May 1st. The Communist Youth Movement made it clear to Leipzig students that they had to participate in the May demonstrations. None of them should entertain any idea of staying at home with their parents.

The day before our departure, I met, by chance, the secretary of the Communist Youth Movement of my student group. He wanted to be sure that I participate in the Leipzig demonstrations. He was speechless when I told him that I had better things to do. I told him that I was going to be in Prague on May 1st. I am sure that my reply was recorded in the "Kaderakte", the confidential personal files which existed for every citizen of East Germany. This incident was, for me, an example of the continuing, almost naïve, self confidence that the reform movement in Prague aroused, not only in me but in many other students who opposed the regime.

In the evening of April 30th, Lothar and I arrived in Prague. We managed to find a room in a student hostel. May Day, which happened to fall on Wednesday that year, was a beautifully sunny day. It was supposed to be the most beautiful May Day Prague had ever seen in this century. The city was excited. Tens of thousands of visitors came early in the morning to the center of town. The Wenzels Square was overflowing with people wanting to take part in the parade. The presence of the international press, including that of Western radio and television journalists, was impressive. Lothar and I waited at Wenzels Square to see how things would develop.

Late that morning, the large demonstration parade headed by Alexander Dubcek, the white-haired President Swoboda and the ministers of the government, reached Wenzels Square. We joined the group a few rows behind Dubcek and walked through the streets of the center of town.

All of a sudden Lothar gave me a push and pointed to the side street where a group of men carried a gallow with a puppet hanging from the top and wearing the uniform of a Soviet soldier. Many people cheered at the sight of this grim scene.

"Wow, that is unbelievable," said Lothar, who did not quite know how to react. I was shocked to see the gallows. It was immediately clear to me what that meant. Obviously a part of the reform movement went out of control. This was a direct assault against the Soviet Union. Under no circumstances would the leadership in Moscow tolerate this. From that moment on, I had a premonition of what would follow.

I looked to the other side of the street and saw a few men whose deliberately inconspicuous clothing I recognized immediately and who kept taking photos of the demonstrators arriving for the main parade.

"Lothar, they look like men from the STASI from East Germany. Let's get out of here. Who knows what will happen if someone recognizes us in these photos."

We left the demonstration parade and went back to Wenzels Square. At that moment, I realized that my conduct was actually illogical since I had told people in Leipzig that I would go to Prague for the May Day Parade. But when I saw the gallow, my self-confidence, my trust in the success of the reform, was suddenly gone. Not that I was afraid, but I had my doubts. The happy mood had completely disappeared.

"Are you aware what this might lead to?" I asked.

"Nothing is clear to me," answered Lothar. "But I admit that by parading the Red Army puppet they went too far."

"I am afraid that this will be the last May Day being celebrated this way here in Prague. Moscow will not be snubbed again."

"What else should they do? Should they have the Red Army march into Czechoslovakia? There'll be a massacre and it will lead to a war with the Americans. No, I don't believe the Russians can afford that."

"Maybe you're right, I hope so. But I am skeptical."

In the evening of that memorable day, we were with friends in the house of Josef Huelle, an engineer, whom we had met a short time ago and who was actively involved in the reform movement. Later that evening, he accompanied us to our quarters. When we said goodbye we agreed to meet again in the summer. I had no idea that it would take two decades until we would see each other again. Only in 1986, I met Josef, who now calls himself Joe, again in his house, at Lake Tahoe, California, where he and his wife are now living.

The following morning, we left Prague. We took the train to Dresden where Lothar and I parted company. I wanted to spend the weekend with my parents in Reinsdorf.

It was unusually warm for that time of the year. On Sunday morning when the sun came out, I decided to take a motorcycle trip to the Erzgebirge Mountains. The journey led me to Hartenstein, then to Aue and then onto the mountains, the ridge of which formed the border line with Czechoslovakia.

East of Johanngeorgenstadt, I came close to the border. I traveled on a gravel road through the woods near Oberwiesenthal. From earlier motorcycle excursions I remembered that this path went directly to the border.

Suddenly, I was stopped by a Red Army patrol, which had put up a temporary barricade. Although my Russian was not too good, I began a conversation with the Soviet soldiers. I learned from them that the border zone had been closed for the last two days. They said that it was a routine military action. I became somewhat suspicious. I knew that the Soviet Army units held military exercises together with the East German Army ever so often. Years ago I took part in such a military exercise near the Polish border. But I had never heard that these exercises were held in early May.

The soldiers offered me one of their Papirossi cigarettes, which I reluctantly smoked, and proceeded to tell me that this was a big exercise involving many units and tanks. I thought it peculiar that they would divulge such details since they were usually not allowed to give any details to outsiders. I could only think that when they were stationed in East Germany, they never talked to any citizen of East Germany. This was understandable because most people spoke little or no Russian. They were not enthusiastic to learn the obligatory Russian language in school.

When they realized that I could make myself reasonably understood in their mother tongue, the soldiers became very friendly, even more so when I told them about my trips to Moscow and Leningrad a year earlier.

A little later, I returned by the forest road I came from, but for only a short distance. I parked my motorbike behind some bushes and went on foot back in the direction of the border. First, I walked not too close to the road and then turned to go directly towards the border. I reached a clearing with several fields. Now I could see with my own eyes what the soldiers had told me. Not far from the Czech border were hundreds of soldiers who had established themselves in tents and trailers. I could also see tanks and canons.

A few days before, when listening to BBC, I heard that an unusually big military exercise was to be held close to the Czech border. These exercises were coupled with a probable invasion into Czechoslovakia by soldiers of the Warsaw Pact. The BBC radio announcer stressed the point that it was only speculation and that there were no indications of an imminent invasion. But nevertheless, the sight of Soviet soldiers there was reason for reflection.

The experience at the Czech border still occupied my thoughts when I arrived on the following day in Leipzig. I discussed this with my friends. Finally we agreed not to over-rate the situation. Someone in our group mentioned that he heard that units of the Warsaw Pact were also going to have military exercises in the summer, just a few weeks away. The troop movements I saw at the Czech border were probably nothing but preliminary exercises.

It was only months later that they turned out to be something much bigger. The military exercises were preparations for the invasion in the August 1968.

Destruction of the Church — May 1968

The day after my return from Prague, I again heard a rumor that had reached me months before. The old university, the Augusteum and the St Paul's University Church might be blown up. When I heard this for the first time, I did not take it all that seriously. To blow up one of the oldest and best-preserved churches of East Germany would be utter madness. Not even the Ulbricht government would dare to do such a thing. Some time ago, the party officials headed by Mr Froehlich, the SED regional secretary, demanded the demolition of the University Church and the Augusteum; but they could not prevail with the government headquarters in Berlin.

When the SED party chief Ulbricht several times criticized the slow pace of rebuilding the city center of Leipzig, Mr Froehlich felt that he was being criticized; therefore, he ordered the rebuilding of Karl-Marx Square. His motto was: "This square will be the most beautiful square in all of Europe."

In the spring of 1968 there were five different ways that could be chosen for rebuilding the Western section of the square. Only one concept included St Paul's Church, that of an architect from Rostock. All other plans had the church and the Augusteum removed.

It was clear from the beginning that the SED party would like to see the church removed. It had been a thorn in their eyes for years, because traditionally the opposition groups would meet there. By demolishing the church, the SED wanted to strike at the heart of the Leipzig opposition movement.

It took the citizens of Leipzig, the general public of East Germany, as well as the international community by surprise that the party bosses had chosen the sketches of the Berlin architect Professor Henselmann, who had built the Stalin Allee in Berlin, and that of the Leipzig city architect Siegel. Shortly after the choice was made, an unparalleled press PR began. No one thought of asking the opinion of the people of Leipzig, who always found St Paul's University Church and the Augusteum a piece of the familiar past which should be preserved. On May 7, 1968 the party officials including Ulbricht held a meeting at which they decided that the church and the Augusteum should be demolished.

The SED party leaders in Berlin and Leipzig had the audacity to have the decision to demolish these important cultural monuments approved by a Leipzig Municipal gathering. This happened on May 23, 1968. VIPs were invited, including the former vice-chancellor of the university, Professor Georg Mayer. He was picked up early in the morning at his home, so that he would not have time to go to the local bar, have a good drink, and possibly forget what he was supposed to say.

The following morning, Mrs Hempel came into my room, excitedly holding the Leipzig newspaper in her hand. "I can't believe it. Read what they say. And they call themselves the government — they are rascals, crooks all of them!"

I quickly read the editorial which announced the planned demolition. The article closed with the following words: May 23 will enter into Leipzig's history as a significant day.

And that was exactly what happened. What happened on that day in the Leipzig City Hall was a miserable act, without parallel in Germany's history. Although members of the municipal authority knew fully well that the citizens of Leipzig were against demolition, they agreed to have the University Church and the

Augusteum destroyed. Paul Froehlich did not feel embarrassed when he explained at the City Hall meeting: "We acknowledge all comments and advice which were sent in from Leipzig citizens and from the entire country." Such cynicism is hard to match.

One delegate, whose name was Sorgenfrei (the name means "without worries") said, "We won't defeat capitalism by restoring and refurbishing old buildings, but we will defeat it with the most recent realizations of science and technology."

The delegate Dr Ullmann of the East German CDU party did not blush when declaring, "In the name of the city delegates belonging to the CDU, I want to acknowledge my appreciation and recognition for the excellent achievement of the participating architects and experts."

The author Erich Loest later wrote about the members of the city government in his book "Voelkerschlachtdenkmal". "What could have happened had they voted against the demolition? Would they have ended up in jail, or would their pension be taken away? Jail, probably not; pension taken away, probably. Today, everyone in Leipzig likes to say that those were wild times. It was Ulbricht and Froehlich who had the Church destroyed but *all* the delegates who were in the municipal government in 1968 are *guilty*. Their entire meeting was an assembly of buggers."

There was growing unrest in the city and its surrounding areas. The example of Alexander Dubcek in Prague set a precedent. The Parliament in Berlin and the Leipzig Municipal delegates generated a dangerous situation with their decision.

Initially, the communist leadership in Leipzig had planned to blow up the church in July. But when they saw how the protest grew, they realized they had to act quickly. Another reason for expediency was the urging by Ulbricht. When Susanne and I arrived at the Karl-Marx Square on the afternoon of May 23, along with many other people, we had to watch helplessly as the area around the university and the church was being cordoned off.

The police task force was at hand at the square minutes after the decision of the delegates was finalized. That evening, just a few hours after the City Hall meeting, the first holes for insertion of explosives were drilled into the walls of the church, the same church that had survived seven centuries of endangerment and wars.

There were demonstrations downtown on the evening of May 23 and the following days. Every evening, Susanne and I went near the Karl-Marx Square. From the steps of the Opera House we witnessed a scene I will never forget — and which reminded me so much of a scene from the movie "Panzerkreuzer Potemkin" by Sergej Eisenstein. A large agitated crowd of about two hundred accumulated in front of the Opera House, including about 50 spies of the Secret Police. All of a sudden, a unit of the police marched in and a brawl began. Finally, I heard an order given and the armed police marched in close formation towards the demonstrators. People fled, a young woman with a baby carriage fell, and the child fell out onto the pavement and cried. The police marched relentlessly over the woman and the baby — injured, both remained on the ground.

We stayed downtown until midnight. Leipzig presented an unusual picture in those days. The city was swarming with strangers, who were obviously from the Secret Police. It seems that the government got all available STASI units of East Germany together and sent them to Leipzig. In the suburbs, members of the army and special units of the Secret Police were not overlooked. Armored vehicles characterized the scene: they were prepared for all eventualities.

I began to think about possible protest actions. It was clear that the demolition could not be stopped, but I felt it was necessary to at least point out to the party leaders that there were forces among the citizens who were willing and able to articulate opposition against the insane order given by Berlin. But what could be done with limited resources and opportunity?

Whenever I was in Leipzig I met my cousin Guenter Fritzsch. He was a bit older than I and two years ahead of me in his physics studies, but we had many friends in common. I often attended discussions held in his flat. He had finished his studies in the meantime and was working on his PhD in biophysics at the university.

Guenter had connections to circles of the church in Leipzig, mainly through his future father-in-law, who was pastor in the Gholis quarter of Leipzig. He told me about the outrage among the clerics and people close to the church.

Often, I also saw Stefan Welzk, a student friend of Guenter's. I had come to know him a couple of years before, when he was a teaching assistant having to correct my homework in theoretical physics.

Stefan chose to study physics because of the intellectual challenge which this work would entail. Basically, his main interest was literature and philosophy. His extraordinary memory allowed him to recite endless passages from poems by Bertold Brecht, Georg Heym, Gottfried Benn and others. He shared a large apartment with his father in Gohlis. The flat would have been a true goldmine for the Secret Police with all the literature that endangered the state's attitude.

Stefan provided me with all the literature in the forbidden list that we were thirsting for. He gave me books by Camus and Sartre, and George Orwell's "1984", which I was allowed to keep only for 24 hours. Susanne and I read the book together in one night. Through Stefan's connection I was able to read the forbidden poems by Bertold Brecht and Gottfried Benn and last, but not least, current West German journals.

Now back to the demolition of the church. When the decision to demolish the church became public, an immediate outcry came from everywhere. The theological faculty and seminary of the university went openly against the demolition. Many protest letters reached Mayor Kresse who went all out in support of the destruction of the church. The President and the government of West Germany in Bonn protested in vain. The last sermon in St Paul's Church was held on May 23, which happened to be Ascension Day, to a packed house.

After that, one could only enter the church with a special permit. Church dignitaries were able to save a few valuable artifacts at the last minute. I had to think about the many books which I had inspected during my time there working at the library. I also thought about Frau Werner whose "domain" would be gone in a few days. Fortunately, the two most valuable parts of the organ could be disassembled.

The demolition was planned for May 30, exactly one week after the decision was made. The students were told, under threat of punishment, to partake in their studies as usual and under no circumstances were they to go downtown.

Susanne and I decided to ignore this and rode the next day, which was a beautiful sunny May Day, on our bikes downtown. We left our bikes near the Grassi Museum which was about 200 meters east of the Karl-Marx Square. We walked up to the barricade, which was erected in a radius of 300 meters from the location of the detonation by the police. Thousands of Leipzig residents were there. It was swarmed with police and "inconspicuous" Secret Police.

Together with dozens of additional people, which, no doubt included some Secret Police agents, we found a heap of rubble from which we could overlook the Karl-Marx Square. The night before the detonation, fir trees were put against the lower walls of the church and the Augusteum in order to ease the force of the explosion and to minimize the dust development. Also, many empty streetcars had been deposited on Karl-Marx Square in an effort to weaken the shock waves of the explosion.

When it got close to 10 o'clock the bells of all the churches in Leipzig began to ring. Susanne silently looked at me with tears in her eyes. As well as possible, I tried to play the neutral observer who had come to witness the demolition of the old church and university, out of pure curiosity. It was difficult to disguise our anger and despair.

At the first muffled bang Susanne winced. A series of explosions echoed through the streets of Leipzig. The first explosion knocked off the foundation of the church. Having been standing for seven centuries, the church now collapsed; an enormous cloud of dust enveloped downtown Leipzig.

Susanne whispered to me, "I can't believe it. One day this will be avenged. They begin to destroy their own country — our country. This is the beginning of their end."

And she was going to be proven right. Two decades after the demolition, at the same square, the storm began to sweep the East German government away. In that context, the destruction of the University Church had not been in vain. At the same time the wish by the SED Party to hit at the heart of the opposition movement was not granted. St Paul's role as the meeting place for the opposition movement was taken over by Nikolai Church, which was located only 200 meters away.

When the explosions were over, some people around us applauded, others screamed or whistled. A young man shouted, "Criminals!" The Secret Police began to "work" and brawls erupted. An old man who openly verbalized his protest was beaten up and bloodied and put into a car. One person, who had disregarded the strict order not to photograph the demolition of the church, was led away after his camera was whacked out of his hand.

The Secret Police had no idea that only a few meters away, a courageous photographer, Karin Wieckhorst, had photographed all phases of the demolition from a window of the Grassi Museum with a special camera (see illustration).

Susanne and I went to the student cafeteria. Only a few students had had the courage to disregard the ban on witnessing the detonation. You could feel how dampened the mood was among the students on that day. Also, Susanne and I were overcome with hopelessness. I took her home and we spent the evening together. We talked about our future.

"What will happen to our country, what will happen to us?" Susanne looked at me questioningly. "When the church collapsed today, I had to think about these questions. I feel that you don't want to remain here. You will go away, right?"

I drank some wine and looked at her silently. Then I said slowly, "What else should we do? They'll destroy this country totally, the same as what the Nazis did before them. I don't think it makes sense to stay, unless there will be changes like in Prague. But after all that happened here today, I doubt change can happen. Maybe I'll try to escape this year. Then I'll get you out."

"I don't know what I should do," said Susanne. "When everybody who could bring about changes leaves, it'll get worse. Then nothing will ever change. Also, as you know, my mother would never leave her home country."

I nodded. I had spoken with Susanne's mother several times about the possibility of leaving East Germany. She made a gesture of refusal. As a medical doctor she was needed in her home town. And since Susanne had a very close relationship with her mother, it was clear to me that it would be extremely difficult for Susanne to follow me to the West and leave her mother behind with a possibility of never seeing her again.

At midnight I left her apartment and walked slowly to my room, and I sensed that 30 May, 1968 was a decisive point for the direction that my future would take.

The University church St Paul in Leipzig just before
the destruction

The impressive Gotic Arch of the St Paul's Church

The photographer Karin Wieckhorst succeeded in taking a picture
of the church during the destruction with a special camera

A series of explosions halled through the streets of Leipzig ...

... until the seven hundred years old church had disappeared

The transparency, which was painted by Rudolf Treumann, came down on June 20, 1968 at the final concert of the International Bach Festival in the congress hall of Leipzig

The installation at the Augustus square, which indicates the
contours of the previous St Paul's Church

Preparations and a Visit by the Secret Police

Just one day after the university buildings and St Paul's Church had been blown up, I ran into my cousin Guenter. We sat together and talked about the most recent developments, and we agreed on one thing: the destruction of these buildings could not be simply accepted. Some clear demonstration against the communist regime had to be organized so that they would understand that they had gone too far.

"What can we do? Do you have any concrete suggestion?" I asked Guenter.

"We might organize some protest action during an official event. We might unveil a transparency — something like that."

"I thought somewhat along similar lines," he said. "We might roll down a transparency from the gallery of the St Thomas Church, and then run away quickly ..."

"You are truly optimistic. You think we can get away with that?" Guenter asked. "You know that Secret Police are always included in the guest list at every event at St Thomas Church. You wouldn't get very far. Even if we really wanted to take such a chance, we would have to plan it very carefully. Still, the best occasion to have such a demonstration would be at the final concert of the International Bach Competition when some artists will receive prestigious prizes. This competition will happen soon. That concert is seen as a cultural as well as a political event: a lot of bigwigs from the party and from the government will be there."

"That sounds like a great idea. I'll try to think about the details which might make it successful."

On my way home, I thought about the discussion in much more detail. Guenter was right about that this concert was offering a fine chance. But during our discussions I had gained the firm impression that he was willing to contribute ideas, but that he was not willing to be actively involved. I could easily sympathize with him, because fleeing the country was out of the question. Unlike me, he was not an East German citizen "on call", but meant to stay right there.

I asked him about certain details and found out that the final concert was not to be performed, as I anticipated, in St Thomas Church but rather on 20 June in the Congress Hall next to the zoo. At an earlier event I had taken a look at the stage in the Congress Hall and noticed that there was a fire ladder on the right of the stage — a contraption that might be helpful to install transparencies from the flies above the stage.

When I saw Guenter the next day in the dining hall, he took me to the side and asked, "Did you hear about Stefan's news?"

"What news?" I asked. "Did Stefan commit some nonsense?"

"This morning I heard that a large poster was found at St Thomas Church saying: 'To be blown up also'. You may ask three times who put that up."

I had to laugh: "clearly that must have been Stefan, who else?"

Guenter continued, "The Secret Police was on the spot immediately, and this made the rounds in Leipzig in no time flat. The church leaders were afraid it may have meant to be a provocation to the STASI. It's odd enough that neither the church dignitaries nor the SED people caught the humor of that absurd demand. They didn't get it."

"Well, humor and spreading jokes are the last things we tend to suspect the SED to indulge in; and the church people are much too afraid at this point."

I gave a hint that I had some ideas about what to do next, but I didn't want to be specific unless I had first discussed the matter with Stefan alone.

Next morning I went to see him at his place in Gohlis. His father opened the door. Stefan was still asleep, so I tried to crack a joke:

"Get out of bed! If you go on with your posters in German churches, you'll soon have an orderly assignment as an inmate in the penitentiary at Bautzen   that's where they have to get up early. You might just as well get used to it!"

"You might be right," he answered, "but our physique is weak."

"Well, at least I can compliment you on being in bed all by yourself. That counts for extenuating circumstances."

"I'll just as soon do without them."

"Well, get out of bed then, your tasks are waiting to be performed. We need to give Ulbricht a 'slap on his cheek'."

"And that is what you call work? That's nothing but a great pleasure."

And with that remark, he jumped out of bed and we started to get serious. I told him of the plan: as the last concert of the International Bach Festival competition in the Congress Hall comes to its conclusion, a transparency will be very visibly rolled down from above the stage.

"And how do you expect to be able to do that without being commissioned, the same evening, to the lofty position of a squeezed lemon in the basement of the STASI prison?"

"I might be able to do that with a quick mechanical release, and then vanish quickly."

"Nonsense. After all, we are physicists. We simply take an electric switch that is connected to a clock. With that, we need not even be present; the clock will do the job for us."

With the greatest zeal, we got going. Stefan took over the logistics, both of us were fascinated with the technical details; and didn't even think of the risks we were taking.

"So be it." said Stefan, "You'll take care of the switch mechanism and I'll see to the transparency."

"And what will the transparency show? We need somebody who can create a good image, an artist if at all possible."

"I'll take care of that. I am going to Potsdam tomorrow, and we'll take it from there. But we are in a hurry; the concert is only ten days away."

"All right," I said, "I'm going home over the weekend. I'll try and find a useful mechanism in my workshop."

The following weekend I was in Reinsdorf. I still had a little electronics shop at my parent's place, where, as a student, I had gained my first experiences with radios and transmitters. That was where I had put together a simple electrical starter mechanism, to be set in action by a clock. It was strong enough to unroll a heavy transparency at a precisely prescribed time.

I tried my mechanism repeatedly, with limited success. Sometimes it worked, at other times it didn't. The mechanism was not really reliable. After all, we needed a device that would function reliably 100%, not maybe 99% of the time! That was when I recalled having put together, as a little boy, a starter gear that was to do just one thing: switch on the radio in our living room without having to get out of bed. It was a really simple device. I had fastened to the ring of an alarm clock a small turning shaft. As soon as the alarm clock sounded off, this shaft started winding up a thread which was strong enough to change a switch from "off" to "on". That might be my solution!

I borrowed from my mother a big old alarm clock and copied my old switch device. It turned out to be strong enough to pull a big nail which was to hold on to the rolled-up transparency and pull it out of its hole. Everything worked just fine. In my father's big workshop I made a heavy wooden board drop down from the top floor several times with the device. I had solved my problem!

When I saw Stefan again early in the following week, I told him right away, that put him to work. He insisted on not telling me any details, so that, should we run afoul of the police, I could truthfully say I had no knowledge of all this. Only later on, when we had made it to the West, I found out the details.

In a shop in Potsdam that specialized in cloth for flags, he bought a large piece of yellow cloth — about $2.5 \times 5 \ m^2$. In Berlin he looked around for an alarm clock that was as big and sturdy as possible with a very loud ring. He found one in a departmental store in Alexander Square.

Stefan had accepted a graduate fellowship at the Academy of Science in Potsdam, so he commuted frequently between Potsdam and Leipzig. At the Academy he had met a like-minded colleague. His name was Rudolf Treumann. I also knew Rudolf and had occasionally visited him, together with Stefan, at his institute close to the famous Einstein Tower. Rudolf was not exclusively a physicist; he also did painting in his free time. Not only that, he was also interested in music.

When Stefan asked him whether he might paint our transparency, he accepted enthusiastically. His acceptance showed admirable courage. After all, he had a family with two small children, and unlike Stefan and myself, he was not planning to leave East Germany in the foreseeable future.

The job he had just accepted to do in Stefan's room in Potsdam was not an easy one. He had to paint on a rather large piece of cloth in a small room. His landlady was smart enough to get an idea that something was happening in her apartment, which should be kept out of the public. She did a wonderful job of pretending that she knew nothing.

During that period I worked feverishly on the preparation of my examinations. In early May I had told Professor Treder in Potsdam that I was planning to submit my already concluded preliminary study of my PhD thesis as a Master's thesis. That would put at least one initial academic grade on my roster. After all, I was not so sure I would still be in East Germany in fall. And to start serious work in the West, it would be an advantage to have a final degree in my pocket.

Treder mumbled something for himself and then told me, "Frankly, I don't get it. You were supposed to go straight towards your PhD. Why on earth would you go for a Master's? As soon as you have your doctorate, nobody will be interested in a Master's."

"You are right if in fact I stay in the academic world. But who knows what comes next for me? I might wind up in industry, where a Master's degree is appreciated. At any rate, adding that somewhat lower degree cannot be wrong. It doesn't cost me a thing, just that I have to pass the additional exams."

Professor Treder looked at me attentively, and I had a feeling he felt there might be additional motivations on my side. But he told me to go ahead. The relevant exams would be scheduled for late June.

One evening after dinner, when I came home with Susanne, Mrs Hempel had an odd piece of news for me: a man had been there looking for me. She was alarmed.

"Let me tell you this: he did not look like somebody we want to be watched by. Do be careful! He wouldn't take no for an answer, so I told him to come back tomorrow morning."

The next morning I worked at home, the doorbell rang at about ten o'clock. Mrs Hempel opened the door and escorted the visitor to me. We sat down on the sofa of my room. The visitor was about forty years old; he was correctly dressed with a white shirt and a tie. He apologized just in case he interrupted my work, and then came to the point:

"I come from the Regional Party Office; I am responsible for security matters. Please do not be astonished that I come to see you, and please don't be alarmed. We know you are one of the top students at the Physics Institute, and that you are working on your PhD thesis. We also know you are not always of one mind with things that happen in our state. We are aware of your contacts with people in Leipzig who do not agree with all the directives issued by the party. At the same time, we believe you are ambitious, and that you want to advance rapidly in our state. In order to accelerate our progress on the working scale, we need the participation of the broadest possible consensus of our people. I am sure you understand. In order to assure the safety of our state in its combat against Western imperialism, we need to work closely together not only with our party members. Please think about this: Would you like to help us? If so, it will not turn out to be against your advantage. You are all of twenty-five years old; you'll probably get your PhD next year. You might advance quickly in your career; maybe become a professor very soon."

I was dumbfounded. Was this just a trap of the State Security Service, or were they really so shameless as to ask me to become a spy for the state? Obviously, I had to be very careful. I clearly did not understand the whole point, and cautiously evaluated the situation.

"So, what collaboration efforts do you think may be helpful?"

"For starters, you need not do anything at all. If you agree to help us, we'll first talk this over in our main offices, and I'll approach you at a later time."

"That sounds fine. But I would like to know in what form my work would be. After all, I am a scientist, and I don't have much interest in politics. I have a hard time imagining what you might expect from my possible participation in your work."

The functionary smiled when he said, "You know, these matters develop as they go. Let me just give you an example. You work here at the Physics Institute and simultaneously at the Academy in Potsdam. We might, let's say, need to obtain certain information concerning the director of the Institute for Theoretical Physics, Professor Heber, and his collaborators. You might be quite helpful to us in this vein — just as an example. The main point is: we need reliable collaborators on whose flexibility we can rely on. Specific tasks will just pop up. By the way, your contribution will be paid for generously, considering your work."

So that was it: the Secret Service meant to buy my services in this context — to be a spy at the Physics Institute. Not that this was so extraordinary, there were spies in all institutes, and I was well aware that a lot of jobs in East Germany, specifically jobs of professors, were motivated by such activities.

I ran, mentally, down a long list of my friends and acquaintances: was it possible that one of them was already a spy? The consequences of such a possibility would be awful enough to frighten me. In this state, who was still trustworthy? All of a sudden, I noticed that maybe I had acted in good faith too often. In any case, at this point I needed to gain some time.

"I don't really know," I answered. "You'll understand that I've got to think about this a bit."

"Of course," he said, "we know that such decisions don't come easily. There is no hurry. Just tell me when I should come back in order to continue this conversation."

"It's already June. My exams will come soon, and then I would like to take a vacation, so how about early September?"

"Alright, although that may be a little late, but if you think we can't come to an agreement before, so be it. Here is my address, just in case. You can always reach me by phone should you come to a decision before September — a positive decision, I would hope. Good luck for your exams, and I hope you'll enjoy your vacation. And, please, don't mention my visit to anybody — not a word about it! Tell your landlady I am a distant relative of yours, okay?"

I took my visitor to the door, and to avoid any disturbance among my friends, I didn't mention the odd suggestion of the

Secret Service man to anybody — not to Mrs Hempel or to Susanne.

The following day, I asked Professor Heber whether I could talk to him at the Institute. It turns out he was not astonished about the visit of the man from the Secret Police, when I told him about it. I had the impression he had been expecting this kind of spy approach, and that he took it stoically. He finally told me:

"You know, I can't see that as a tragedy. When you live in a state like ours, you have to expect such matters. But I am concerned about you. Try and keep out of it without making a mess of it. I trust that you will come up with some solution."

I thanked him for our conversation and promised to keep him informed. It became clear to me only after I left his office that I might have made a mistake, maybe there was some invisible microphone in Heber's office, and the Secret Police had listened to our talk. I resolved to be much more careful in the future.

Professor Heber had been offered his job in Leipzig in the early 1960s when he was fairly young. He was one of a small number of professors who were not willing to cater unconditionally to the communist party; he soon was seen as one of the few people who could be trusted by students who counted themselves as the opposition of the state. It turned out that, after we left Leipzig, he was transferred to Dresden, where, for several years, he worked at the Technical University. In the mid-1970s, he was permitted to go to a conference in France. He did not return to Dresden. He accepted an offer to head an institute of theoretical physics at Duisburg University, West Germany. After his escape to the West, his colleagues in Dresden voted to relieve him from his position — a fact which established a telling feature of Dresden academia.

To this day, I have not found out the reason why the Secret Police came to establish the contact with me that I described. Maybe they suspected some disloyalty to their system — but it may also be that they hoped to make me part of their operation.

But I think that the East German Secret Police tried to approach most if not all young academics who looked like they might make it to the teaching or professorial staff at universities. Most of the academic instructors in East Germany, who were hired after the big wall was established to separate East and West Germany, were most probably in touch with the Secret Police. At that time it was exceptional at East German universities that anybody would receive a higher academic position for purely competent qualifications unless he was a party member, or did special jobs for them.

It is understandable that the Communist Party in East Germany had a special interest in university circles. After all, instructors in those institutions established through their contacts with the students, with people who would be leaders of the next generation, their influence on them. Nonetheless, the wide-spread corruption of professors and academic officials and advisors in East Germany was unique among the Eastern European countries. In all other countries of this region, except Romania, instructors were granted liberality and freedom of movement, which was not permitted in other sectors of that society. Take Poland, for example, membership in the Communist Party was seen as a disadvantage for a university career.

For some days, the visit of the Secret Police's agent lingered in my thoughts. I had mentioned to him that I meant to make a decision by September, while in reality, I was thinking of fleeing the country in summer. But what would happen if I was still going to be there in September?

By that time, the International Bach Competition had started to keep all the musical venues in Leipzig occupied. At the very start of that competition something happened: a group of Americans who took part in the organ competition moved across town in a demonstration. They carried a large transparency protesting against the blowing up of the University Church. They were the direct victims since the initial plans for the competition included the organ in St Paul University Church as in previous years — and as this one was no longer available, the relevant concerts had to be in St Thomas Church.

On the evening leading up to 20 June, the day of the final concert, I went to see Stefan in Gohlis.

"How is the transparency coming?" I inquired.

"It's right here. You want to see it?"

We unrolled the big bundle of textile and covered a large part of the room floor with it. In order to see it in full, I climbed on a chair to get a better view. I saw a huge drawing of the University Church on a yellow background. To its right there was a big black cross with the year of its demolition in 1968.

Below, it said in large black letters: "We demand reconstruction."

"Well, do you like it?"

"Very much so, it makes no political statement, only asks for a deceptively harmless demand. But that is just the strength of it. How did you manage to get it done? That was a huge amount of work!"

"That's a secret, as is the name of the painter. And let's leave it that way, okay?"

"Alright, I will not ask again. How many people have seen the transparency so far?"

"Just four: the painter, you and me, and one additional person."

I was a bit astonished. Why had Stefan included somebody else?

"And who is the fourth one?"

"That's a secret."

It took many more weeks; we were already in the West, before he told me the identity of the fifth person. Stefan had not been able to refrain from driving, with the finished transparency, to a reliable acquaintance of his — the well-known and somewhat outlawed poet Peter Huchel, who lived not far from Potsdam. In his garden, he had unfolded the transparency. Huchel, the usually relaxed old man, was very happy and excited when he saw it, and with good reason. Finally, there was going to be a challenge to the Communist regime!

The Transparency

We began to check the release device. Because it was so simple, it functioned extremely well. The alarm clock, of the same size as the one I have at my home, was suited for its task. Stefan had taken the ringer out, and I wanted to know why?

"Let's assume they catch us," Stefan said.

"They could get us for disturbing the concert."

"You can't seriously believe that anyone would hear the ringing of the alarm clock."

"Of course no one would hear it, but you couldn't prove that at a trial."

Stefan had a good point there. In court, they would probably try to prove our action to be criminal rather than political. We needed to prevent that.

Stefan simplified further the release device. It was enough to have the nail, on which the transparency hung on a thin string, put in the opening of the screw from the top of the alarm clock. With the first rotation of the screw, the nail would, through its dead weight of the rolled-up transparency, unroll. We examined and tried the mechanism several times. It was functioning perfectly.

The next day I drove to Gohlis. Stefan had prepared everything. The transparency had been rolled into a 2.5 meter long package that was wrapped in black cloth. At the corners you could see a tripod, so it looked like a technical device. Finally, Stefan put on grey work clothes.

"You look like a telephone technician," I mocked, and acted like I had not a care in the world, which was far from what I really felt. I knew that this action could end in a total fiasco.

"I don't only look like one, I am one; and you know, my firm is sending me to an urgent mounting job in the Congress Hall. See you soon."

Stefan took the streetcar with his bulky luggage directly to the Congress Hall near the Zoo. I followed him on my bike. When he arrived at the Hall he waited across the street. I went into the Hall and looked around. A number of workers prepared everything for the concert that night. They needed to put down cables, put up cameras and microphones. Of course there were the obligatory Secret Police. I went back to Stefan.

"Everything seems to be normal. I'll wait across the street. Be careful! Don't take risks."

"Remember, if something goes wrong, scram. Don't be alarmed, they'll get nothing out of me. I'll say it was all my idea."

Stefan disappeared in the foyer of the Congress Hall with the large black roll. I went to the other side of the street and walked back and forth, keeping my eyes glued to the entrance. I had put my bike close by so that I could quickly leave if necessary. My inner tension increased by the minute.

Although everybody in the Congress Hall could see the long black roll that Stefan was bringing in, no one took notice. Everybody thought this was another device needed for that evening, which was basically correct. Workers were busy on the stage. Stefan opened up a way through the equipment and began to climb the fire ladder to the gridiron. It looked chaotic upstairs. There was a 1-cm high coat of dust everywhere. Apparently, no one had been up here for a long time.

He hung the rolled-up transparency above the middle of the stage, along with the alarm clock. He had planned to wear gloves so he would not leave any fingerprints behind, but that was impossible. The gloves were too small. After a few minutes of work, the transparency was mounted. Stefan was just about to leave when he examined everything again, just as a precaution. Luckily he did, because he realized that the transparency hung inverted with the illustration backwards.

Finally, he was done. The transparency hung correctly and the alarm clock ticked. Stefan engaged the timer to eight minutes past eight o'clock. That was 38 minutes after the beginning of the concert. We chose this time because we believed that at that time all the prizes were handed out and the concert would have started. That was the wrong assumption as we later found out.

When Stefan was downstairs again, he realized that he was covered with dust and was dirty all over. He reached the bathroom quickly in order to get rid of most of the dust. Without being noticed, he was able to leave the Congress Hall half an hour after he had entered it. I breathed out a sigh of relief when I saw him appear at the entrance. Without being too conspicuous he crossed the street and came towards me:

"Everything is okay. The transparency is hanging and the alarm clock is ticking. Now we can only wait. By the way, what are we doing this evening?"

"I thought we should go to the concert. In any case, I got two tickets."

"Are you out of your mind? Do you want to run into the arms of the Secret Police?"

"Why? There will be thousands of people. We wouldn't be noticed. And anyhow, I want to see if the action comes off perfectly."

"You must have a death wish. Then go alone, I don't care. Maybe it's not a bad idea if one of us is there. I mounted the transparency, so it's up to you to witness its effect. It is also more dangerous for me since actually I should be at the institute today. Let's meet after the concert." We arranged to meet at 10:30 pm at the 'Ring'.

That evening I went to the Concert Hall in great anticipation. I met my cousin Guenter and his fiancée in the entrance hall. We said hello and I whispered to him:

"Do pay attention at eight minutes past eight o'clock."

Guenter looked at me startled and whispered back:

"So you did…?"

I nodded and left. My seat was in one of the last rows. Punctually at 7:30 the event started. We had assumed that the prizes would be given out right away, but that wasn't so. First, the Minister of Culture of East Germany spoke for quite a long time. Only then did they start handing out the prizes. The director of the music conservatory, Professor Fischer, an elderly, near-sighted man, did the honors, and that took up some time.

It was already a few minutes past eight o'clock, my heart began to pound faster. Just a few more minutes, these minutes seemed like eternity. He was about to give the prize for the piano and for the organ competition. Among the winners were two Americans who, a few days before had protested against the destruction of the University Church in Leipzig. Finally all the prize winners were on stage, the applause ebbed, and director Fischer wanted to speak again.

Eight minutes past eight o'clock. I watched the stage spell bounded. Quickly, as if steered by the hand of a ghost, the transparency unrolled, and hung there for all to see. I felt how my neighbor to the right twitched. There it was, the picture of the destroyed University Church, with the inscription: 'We demand reconstruction'.

Applause roared and increased to a storm. Some of the concert goers stood up. The near-sighted director Fischer stood helplessly on the stage and could not understand the roaring applause. He was unable to see the transparency since he stood directly underneath it. The party officials, Mayor Kresse and two ministers from Berlin were perplexed. The applause grew even stronger; there were whistles, and many stomped with their feet. Flashlights lit up, press photographers and journalists took pictures. A television team from Japan and one from Czechoslovakia recorded the scene. I watched as people got up and left their rows — possible Secret Police, remembering their duty. I looked at my watch. The applause held six minutes before it ebbed. There were still some whistles audible. A general unrest seized the audience.

Finally, someone reached the upstairs on the dusty fire ladder and lifted the transparency, but it rolled down again right away, releasing a huge dust cloud. Again enthusiastic applause from the Leipzig audience, and again, whistles and shouts were heard. Once again the transparency hung for another half minute before it was heaved up slowly accompanied by whistles and shouts. And now instead of the transparency there was nothing left but a huge speck of dirt. I looked around and everybody was beaming and whispering to their neighbors.

My neighbor, an old gentleman, smiled at me and said: "Splendid, that I could witness this." Although I stayed serious until then, I had to smile, and I relaxed a bit.

The concert continued without any further incidents. I was still excited and had a hard time concentrating on the music. Until now the entire action was more like a student prank, with political background, of which people in the West would only smile. The explosive power of the action suddenly became clear to me. From this evening on there would be no peace, because the Secret Service would not stop until they found the culprit. From now on there was no way out except to escape. The dice had fallen.

The concert ended before 10 o'clock since there was no intermission. There were men at the exit doors screening everyone leaving. I turned to the other side and left. At the streetcar stop across the street I saw Guenter and his fiancée. I strolled towards them and whispered: "Went well, didn't it?"

He gave me a jab in the ribs and said: "Be quiet, not another word."

Luckily, Guenter's fiancée did not hear our little exchange. In view of the fact that the Congress Hall was now surrounded by Secret Police, my comment to Guenter had been a bit careless; fortunately there were no consequences.

At the agreed time I met Stefan. When I described to him how successful our action was, he burst into jubilation, and he was a bit regreted that he had not been there. In a small restaurant we celebrated our success.

When I arrived at home shortly before midnight, Frau Hempel was waiting for me. Her neighbor was at the concert and had already told her what had happened. But now she wanted to hear details from me. Of course, Frau Hempel had no idea that one of the authors of the action was standing in front of her. We drank a cognac together, and then she said: "You know, sometimes I was ashamed for being a resident of Leipzig. Whenever I heard that the criminal with the goatee, the head of the East German Party was from the Eastern part of Leipzig, I was ashamed. Tonight, finally I can be proud. Let's drink to the people responsible for today's transparency, and that many more actions like his will follow until the whole decayed state falls apart like a house of cards. And I tell you, Harald, when that happens; I hope that the people of Leipzig will have a part in it. Cheers!"

And so I drank, with mixed feelings, also to my health.

The Following Days

The story about the transparency spread like wild fire through East Germany. That same evening, several Western news channels and news channels from other countries talked about the event. One journalist erroneously reported an incident took place in the Congress Hall, saying that a bomb had been detonated with the aid of the switch of a clock.

Later we heard about the circumstances not in our favor. Paul Froehlich, Secretary of the East German Party in Leipzig, who was chosen as a possible successor by Ulbricht, next to Honecker, was not at the concert. When he heard right afterwards what had happened at the concert, he went into a rage and demanded an immediate arrest of the culprits. That was not a simple task, but it brought on a commotion among the State Security Service and the police.

Rumors had it that Froehlich had a major heart attack from which he never really recuperated. The party officials kept this, of course, a secret. Several months later, Froehlich actually succumbed. Next to Ulbricht he was one of the party officials who were one of the most ruthless tyrants in East Germany. He had incarcerated hundreds of people for years, and drove some of them to suicide. He had "cleaned up" the university, driving Ernst Bloch and Hans Mayer into exile. The demolition of the church and the university was his last act.

Ulbricht was notified straightaway about the protest action. He gave orders to give it the highest priority finding the people responsible and making them pay. The mechanism of the State Security Service machinery was put into the highest gear.

At that time Ulbricht may have been thinking about his successor. Since Froehlich would not be available due to his illness, the road to the top job in East Germany was now open to Honecker. In all probability it was better for East Germany that Honecker and not Froehlich would succeed Ulbricht. East Germany, under Honecker, experienced in the 1970s a considerable economic upswing. The worst excesses of political oppression by the police and Secret Service were removed. Only in the 1980s did the political pressure increase again. Had Froehlich been in charge, the development would have been worse — he would have maximized the dictatorial behavior of Ulbricht, ruining the country completely, just as it was a short time later under Ceausescu in Romania.

When I was at the university cafeteria with Susanne the day after the concert, I told her about the transparency in the Congress Hall. Of course, I did not mention my role in that action.

We ate at a long table alone until two of my student colleagues saw us and joined us. Not so much on my account, but rather, they were curious about my beautiful female companion. I knew that one of them was probably a Secret Police spy, and the other one was an active member of the party. Suddenly, someone behind me called out my name, came to our table, and slapped on my shoulder. He was a friend from the German philology department I had not seen for quite some time. He was always in a good mood and he did not take things too seriously.

"Hey, Harald, what happened yesterday at the Congress Hall could have had your signature."

I almost choked on my food. Susanne later told me that I turned white as a sheet, and looked like I would collapse any minute. The person opposite from me at the table winced when the Congress Hall was mentioned. I acted as though I had choked on my food; I repeatedly coughed before saying:

"Oh, it's you, next time give me a warning before you hit me on my shoulder while I'm eating. What are you talking about? Do you mean the concert last night, and the transparency?"

"Of course, what else? The entire city is talking about it. Do you have any inkling of who could have done it? It was probably someone from the theology department. I heard last night that they got a bunch of theology students out of bed. When they catch the culprit — watch out, something bad is going to be in store for them."

I tried to change the subject: "How are you? When are you finally taking your exams?"

"Things are taking in their stride. The mills in the German philology department turn slowly but surely. Don't you worry. Well, bye, until the next time."

I breathed a sigh of relief. I hope that all had gone well. The person seated across from me looked at me attentively. I went into the offensive by telling them in detail of my visit at the concert and especially about the transparency. I spoke like a neutral observer of that evening. He must have assumed that I was an indifferent concert visitor at the Congress Hall.

Susanne and I got up shortly after that, rode our bikes towards the university quarter. In front of the Institute of Anatomy was a little park where we sat down on a bench.

"Harald, what happened at the cafeteria just now, that was really strange. Are you sure you had nothing to do with the transparency? You went all white and I had the feeling that something was wrong with you."

"Nonsense, Believe me, I had nothing to do with it."

"Okay, let's assume I believe you. You certainly would be capable of it." And off she went to the anatomy laboratory.

I could not forget what had happened at the cafeteria. Was my fellow student indeed suspicious? And if so, would he tell? Again, fear crept up, and not only for me. Susanne could possibly also be in danger.

I never found out whether my fellow student, who was a very intelligent student and a trained observer, ever thought that I had something to do with the transparency. If so, he did not report me. Not every Secret Police spy was a traitor.

That afternoon I heard more details. By chance, the transparency came down at the moment when the pianist and the organist received their prizes. Therefore, the Secret Police assumed that there must be a connection between the transparency action and the American organist. They thought it could only have been done by someone who knew the exact timing of the evening's event. Next to the Secret Police, only church people had knowledge of the event schedule. The first arrests and interrogations were geared towards students and docents of the theological faculty.

That information depressed me immensely. The idea of innocent people being interrogated and also incarcerated for a short time is not what I wanted to happen. On the other hand, that meant that the Secret Police was, for the time being, on the wrong track. But Stefan and I knew that it was just a matter of time before they got on the right track. A race with time had thus begun.

That evening I met Stefan, and for the first time we discussed what might happen if the Secret Police were on to us.

"You were in Bulgaria last year with Lothar," Stefan said. "He told me that you investigated several escape possibilities."

After I told Stefan everything I knew, he said, "It doesn't sound too bad to go by folding canoe across the Black Sea into Turkey. I suggest you take your exams quickly and we'll travel to Bulgaria at the end of July in order to look into it. Maybe it works. If not, I'll try to escape across the Baltic Sea in the summer."

Farewell to Leipzig

From now on Stefan and I kept ourselves busy working on the details of our trip to Bulgaria. We applied for the necessary travel papers with the authorities and used a fictional private address in Bulgaria. Without giving an address we would not get the travel papers. To give a fictional address was in itself already an offence against the travel laws. If we were caught, it would mean several months in jail.

I examined my folding canoe and bought extra parts such as an outboard motor. There was no opportunity to test the motor before our departure. In order to see whether the motor worked at all, I tried it out on Mrs Hempel's balcony. After several attempts the motor roared like a wild animal. I had a hard time with it. Since the gear unit did not have to get past water resistance, the motor quickly went into high gear. Finally, I figured out how to turn it off, and the motor was quiet. Mrs Hempel came running to the balcony, startled by the tremendous noise. The neighbors also looked out of their windows. After this less than perfect start, I packed the motor. Not until we reached Bulgaria did we try it out again, and it worked beautifully.

I finished my final exams in late June. After that, I had de facto earned my diploma. I would get the certificate only in September.

Susanne and I drove several days in a row out to "Rheinsberg". We were lucky because the weather was kind to us. The afternoon of our last day at the canal I again discussed a possible escape with her. She knew that Stefan and I were to travel soon to Bulgaria, and that this trip was planned in order to get more information for a later escape. The possibility of taking this trip together was never discussed before, because Susanne had to remain in Leipzig the entire summer for her lab work. I tried again to convince her to leave East Germany, and spoke about a new beginning in West Germany or in the United States.

"I believe you are taking it very lightly, Harald," she countered. "I know I have no right to reproach you. Every person should be free to choose where to go. It's bad enough that this is impossible in our country. Take my mother as an example. She could have gone to West Germany a long time ago, before the wall was built. She would have been a successful medical doctor there now. Do you understand: to be here with her patients in her home town, she considers that her duty, her life. And I think the same way. Please do stay here. Every one of us is needed. If all free and independent thinkers were to leave, then nothing would improve in this country."

I knew these arguments only too well. I had discussed them often with my cousin Guenter. He was also determined to remain in East Germany, patiently waiting for better times. I was silent for a while. After all, there was the new movement in Prague. But I felt that there was not really a chance there. Should the Soviet Army strike, it would be in this summer. In addition, I had to reckon daily with the possibility of an arrest because of the protest action and my work in the opposition.

"Let's assume I would be pursued by the Secret Police, should I wait until they appear in my apartment some early morning to arrest me?"

"Why do you ask? That would be different. In that case, it is clear what you would have to do. You should leave immediately. Do you believe I would like you to be incarcerated for years in the Bautzen prison?"

"Would you then join me, or, if that is too dangerous, would you follow when I could help from the West?"

Susanne looked at me attentively. "What is the matter with you? Tell me honestly. Did you do something they could get you for? Were you involved after all in the matter of the transparency? For some time I felt that you were keeping a secret from me."

"No, no, that is all only hypothetical. But there is a possibility that the Secret Police will be aware of me, or may even be already. After all, I did several things that would be enough for a conviction — take our political meetings, or our connections with Prague. It only takes one spy in our midst."

"If you go to the West, I would probably follow if at all possible. But I hope this is not the case. But for now, let's go swimming, the last time today. Who knows when we'll be here again the next time?"

And indeed, this was to be the last time at "Rheinsberg" for us. Stefan and I decided to travel to Bulgaria in mid-July. A week before that I went to the dean's office to get the certificate of my diploma. That was important because with this certificate I was allowed to change more money than under normal circumstances. When I got the certificate, I suddenly had an idea: "There is something else; could you please also put down the grades on the certificate?"

"Why? In a few weeks you'll get your documents which contain all your grades. Do you think anyone at the bank is interested in the grades of your graduation?"

"I know, but my parents are interested in my final grades. I'm going home tomorrow and for that reason I would love to show my grades to them."

The secretary, an elderly lady, gave me a searching look. Without a word she took the certificate and typed in the grades and then handed the stamped paper back to me. She smiled, "Well, I believe that is enough for your parents. I wish you a good journey, goodbye until September. Keep in mind that you have to pick up your diploma in person. It won't work through the mail."

Leaving, I looked back. The secretary gave me a friendly nod. It was clear, she suspected the reason that I needed the grades for.

Later it turned out that the certificate from the dean's office was very useful, since the Secret Police confiscated my diploma after my escape. I never received it. Instead, the harmless certificate issued by the dean's office was presented to the National Bank of East Germany and which accidentally got damaged in the sea water during the escape, together with Stefan's declaration in lieu of an oath, served me as a substitute for the official diploma. Should the dean's secretary ever read these lines, I would like to express my belated gratitude to her.

The evening before my departure to my parents' home, there was a concert at the Congress Hall. Susanne and I went there. After the intermission Swjatoslaw Richter with the Gewandhaus Orchestra played the piano concerto in D-minor by Sergei Rachmaninov. I got the tickets especially because I knew that Susanne loved this particular piano concerto.

After the concert we drove to the "Voelkerschlachtdenkmal" (war memorial monument) as we had done so often before. At night we had the monument all to ourselves. Susanne always thought that this colossal monument could only be found beautiful at night. This time the big dome with the figures was extremely impressive in the moonlight. We sat down on a bench in front of the monument and talked for a long time. It was late when we finally got back to Susanne's apartment.

The next morning we discussed our plans for the fall term as though I would return in September. Although I was officially no longer a student in Leipzig, but a PhD candidate in Potsdam, I kept my room at Mrs Hempel's for at least a year until after the graduation. In this way I could be in Leipzig often. After that, we would have to see.

Now it was time for the farewell ...

It was hard for me not to tell Susanne about Stefan's and my escape plan. But it would be too dangerous to include her in these plans. Had it been established that she had knowledge of our escape plans, she might have wound up in prison for years.

A few days before the departure I cleaned my room in Leipzig. Everything suspicious, especially unauthorized books, I had removed. Should the escape be successful, the Secret Police would leave no stone unturned in my room — that was certain. I had to be sure that no papers with addresses of friends and acquaintances would be found. On the top shelf in the cupboard I put the address of the Secret Police agent who had visited me. I wrote on that paper: call beginning of September, important. Who knows, this piece of paper could serve as a small alibi.

I had said my goodbyes with friends. I wanted Lothar to understand clearly that I was serious this time about my intention to escape and promised to keep him abreast of my situation. He wanted to wait for another year so that he could finish his diploma before having to decide whether he would stay or not. I also told my cousin Guenter that I would possibly not return. He understood. He knew that sooner or later the Secret Police would arrest us because of the transparency action in the Congress Hall.

It was almost noon when I returned home from Susanne's apartment. I said good-bye to Mrs Hempel who wished me a wonderful vacation and a healthy return in September. Then I traveled on my motorcycle towards Zwickau.

At the Golden Beach

I had only a few days at my parent's place in Reinsdorf. Those days were filled with various preparations for the trip to Bulgaria. My mother helped and prepared a large canvas for my folding canoe. In my mind I said farewell to my home. I tried to fill my memory with details, and I visited friends and school buddies. The day before my departure I took a ride on my motorcycle through the nearby Erzgebirge mountains.

My parents and siblings had no idea about my escape plans. I put my boat as check-in luggage at the train station directly to Varna. Since it was forbidden to take an outboard motor abroad, I hid it in my hand luggage. In the late afternoon my train left Zwickau. In Dresden I had to change to the night train to Prague. I anticipated the border control with tense feelings. It certainly would mean problems and endless interrogations should they find the motor. But the border police left me in peace. I arrived early in the morning in the Czech capital city, on schedule.

A few hours later, the train from Leipzig arrived. Stefan got out of the train with lots of luggage and two gasoline canisters which he had found in Potsdam. I felt very relieved when I saw them, because the canisters were very important. I myself had been unable to get them, for years they had been a scarce commodity in East Germany.

We traveled the same route I had taken the year before with Lothar. After two days we reached Varna. Exhausted, we took the bus to Druzba with our luggage. Once there, we went directly to the camping ground — the same one that I had seen a year before. It took no time to put up our little tent, and we were able to get some good sleep. Next day, Sunday 14 July 1968, I read the headline in the paper: Military exercises in Czechoslovakia by the troops of the Warsaw Pact were successful and had come to an end.

We spent the following day at the beach talking about the details of what to do next. In order to fool the East German officials and to protect our relatives, we each wrote a postcard home, telling them about our vacation stay at the coast.

The next day we retrieved our boat from the rail freight at the station. This was a bit more complicated than anticipated, since we had to explain to the customs officer that the two large pieces were truly a boat. They had never heard of a folding canoe.

To assemble the boat was no problem. I breathed more easily. Not a single screw was missing. The six-meter long blue boat was a sensation and curious people gathered around. Stefan's first training with the boat — he had never been in a folding canoe before — went well. After several failed landing approaches in heavy sea, we were finally a good team, and ready to take longer outings.

Since we did not know whether the border patrol would be observing the coastline with their telescopes, we decided to take longer tours out to sea on a daily basis, so that they would get used to our activities. Our first outing was without the motor. We paddled about ten kilometers out on a calm sea and utilized the wind to get back. I searched the coast with my binoculars. There was no sign that anyone had followed us. According to my experience from the previous year, I had not expected it.

The following morning I mounted the motor to our boat. I had never used the folding canoe with a motor, but it was working very well. Cockily, Stefan and I went at very high speed parallel to the coast. But we quickly realized that the constant breaking of the waves against the boat was not good for it. The screws and frame loosened and we had to go back to the beach in order to fix the boat. That was a good lesson for us: in order to go on for hours with the motorized canoe at high breakers, we had to adjust our speed to the speed of the waves. That meant that at high seas we could not go faster than ten kilometers per hour.

On that same afternoon we went far out to sea. The coastline was only scarcely visible at the horizon. Again, there were no problems. An excursion ship passed near us but took no notice of us. We did not see any boats of the coastguard or any warships.

The following day we sailed northeast of Varna to a small fishing village called Balcic which is inhabited by gypsies. We arrived in good shape, but the return was another matter — it was disastrous. The wind got stronger and stronger and we had to go against the waves. We could not use our sails. On top of it, we left the motor in the tent. Therefore, we had to paddle for hours against a strong wind. We just about made it back.

For the first time we got to know the treachery of the Black Sea. The waves in the Bay of Balcic were high and short, which was poisonous for our long, sleek boat. With the greatest of efforts we reached Druzba. People at the beach helped us to bring in the boat. It was almost totally filled with water and it was kept afloat only through the air bubbles attached at the bow and at the stern.

We were really exhausted and depressed. How would we be able to cross the Black Sea towards Turkey if we could not even master a harmless trip to Balcic? The entire venture appeared hopeless. We went to the hot water spring filled with subterranean sulfur located directly by the beach. The hot water felt good. Slowly, we recovered from our difficulties and rekindled new hope: "You know, we shouldn't take this unsuccessful trip too seriously. These horrible short waves, which almost broke our boat, are probably only found here in the Bay of Varna. Out there on the sea, the waves are long and not so dangerous for our boat. Should there be strong winds tomorrow, we'll try it further out anyway."

"Well, maybe you should go alone tomorrow," growled Stefan. "I'm fed up."

The next day we stayed on the beach. Although it was sunny, the wind grew into a storm, and we saw that the sea which had been, until now, rather calm, was developing incredible strength. The sight of huge breaking waves that would destroy our boat in no time flat did not exactly lift our spirit.

"It would almost be easier to cross the green border from Hungary into Yugoslavia rather than getting away across the sea," said Stefan. "In Hungary we end up only in prison. Here, we'll end up as fish food, and that process is not reversible."

"Not to panic, please. We can always go back to Hungary. Now we arc hcrc, and if the escape doesn't work, we'll just vacation here. Tomorrow, we'll see, I am still optimistic. After all, people in the 1920s succeeded in crossing the Atlantic Ocean in a folding canoe."

"Do you have any idea how many adventurers did not make it?"

"I don't have the faintest idea, but I am sure there is no access to precise statistics. And the Black Sea is much smaller than the Atlantic Ocean."

"But also more treacherous," countered Stefan. "Not without reason is it called the Black Sea."

I could not say anything against this argument, and that ended our discussion.

The Escape

Unfortunately, the weather was not much better the next few days. There were constantly strong winds, especially in the early afternoons. Nonetheless, we started our boat exercises every morning and practiced taking out the motorized folding canoe into higher waves. This was an exercise which turned out to be essential later on. We also got to know the weaknesses of the boat and tried to weed them out. We secured all frames with wire in order to increase its stability.

Tuesday, 23 July, the wind subsided noticeably. We had new hope and began the preparations for our departure. In another postcard to my parents I wrote, "As soon as the sea is calmer we will start going south. The next stop will be in Nessebar und Burgas before we go to the mountains. I intend to stay as long as my money lasts, maybe until beginning of September."

I hinted to my parents before my departure that we wanted to spend some time in the mountains after our stay at the coast, and that they might not hear from us for a while. This precautionary measure was well thought out. By showing the postcards to the Secret Police after our escape, my parents could conceivably convince them that they had no knowledge of my escape.

The next day the sea was smooth as glass and the weather report predicted continued beautiful weather conditions. That is when we decided to leave on Thursday, 25 July. Stefan had found out that there would be a new moon on that particular night, which was a useful circumstance in our venture. At the camp site, where we had met a few other campers, we announced that we would try other camping places south of Varna. Should we be caught on the high sea, we could use this announcement as our alibi.

On the evening of the 25th, we celebrated the end of our stay in Druzba with our neighbors in the camp site, including a group of West German students from Stuttgart who were on their way to Turkey. We sat in front of the campfire for quite a while and discussed the recent events in Czechoslovakia. The government of Prague under their leader Dubcek prepared for difficult negotiations with the Soviet leadership which were to begin in the following week in a movie theater of the small village of Cierna nad Tisou, a town at the Soviet border. Nobody foresaw that those negotiations were only a sham. The violent end of the reform movement had already been decided.

We were awakened the next morning by the warm sunray — it was a beautiful day. There was no breeze in the air. Stefan and I started with the many tasks before us. We filled the gasoline canisters, almost 40 liters, at a nearby gas station. We had to stash our entire luggage, including the tent, in the boat, since we were ostensibly going to the next camp site in the south. Our friend, Boris Slavov from Sophia, whom we had called, met us the same morning.

Early afternoon Boris, Stefan and I splurged at a nearby beach restaurant with a substantial meal. In addition to our escape plans, there was another reason to celebrate: it was Stefan's birthday. Finally, around four in the afternoon we were ready. We said our goodbyes to Boris who shook his head constantly and said that he was probably the last person we would see in our live. In his mind we certainly would be victims of the next storm. When we left the small harbor with our packed boat, he waved for a long time. Stefan sat in front, I at the back, giving the directions.

We started in a south-eastern direction and distanced ourselves from the coast only very slowly. After a while we had the large Bay of Varna in front of us. We saw some sailboats. A large steamship crossed our path. We waved, but the crew ignored us. Stefan recited quietly verses by Georg Heym.

I was seized by an eerie calmness. With every meter our boat went away from the shore; I gained more inner space from the world I had spent 25 years in. From now on I would see another part of the world; and I would have no possibility to visit, even on vacation, my old world. This day would mark a decisive turning point in my life. After this, nothing would be as it had been; this was like crossing into a new life.

The calm sea and the cool air had a soothing influence on my spirit. I realized that I was gaining in self confidence and strength. I did not fear a possible storm or the possible demise of the boat; nor did I have second thoughts of being caught on the High Seas. I was certain that our plan would succeed and we would arrive in the West soon.

The boat was gliding over the glassy water; the motor chucked along. I changed our course a little until we went vertically to the coast out to the sea. I wanted to be far from the coastguard boats before it got dark.

Looking to the north, I could clearly see the beacon of Cape Kaliakra, north of Balcic. The beacon aided us to stay on course the entire night. Although we had a small compass, we rarely used it. Mostly, I oriented myself on the beacons of Kaliakra and Varna and also on the positions of the stars. In order to hold the course, I chose a certain star to define the direction of our motion. This, of course, was not an exact method, but was good enough for us, since we did not have an exactly defined destination. We just wanted to go south until we reached the Turkish coast.

Stefan and I had considered going straight across the sea until we would reach the Asian coast of Turkey. But after careful consideration we gave up this plan because it seemed too dangerous. We would be too long on the open sea and would be helpless at the mercy of possible storms. Luckily we made that decision because the route across the sea would have ended in a fiasco due to the storm ahead.

At this point I had to think about the story of an attempted escape by the Russian astrophysicist George Gamov, who was the first to develop a model for the cosmic Big Bang. This escape story was known worldwide among the physicists. In the 1930s he tried to flee in a small sailboat, which was larger than our folding canoe, from the Crimea peninsula towards Turkey. He got into an enormous storm, and at the end he was happy to have been rescued by a Soviet cruise ship. He said that because of the big storm he got off course. With this excuse he was spared punishment. Later on, he left the Soviet Union by taking, as he wrote in a letter to Josef Stalin: "a well-deserved 20-year vacation from the Soviet Union."

Our new plan was to go at a distance of about 100 kilometers parallel to the coast towards south-east until we reached the Turkish coast near the Bosporus. This way we would circumnavigate the police boats located far out at sea. Our dream version was to arrive directly at the mouth of the Bosporus and continue on to Istanbul. Secretly I envisioned the docking at the harbor of Istanbul as if it were routine, and go to the West German Consulate.

Finally, it was totally dark. There was little to see on the surface of the water. I thought it might be similar to being in a space ship in the universe. You would travel into nothing, into a dark empty space.

After a little while our eyes got used to the darkness. I could see very faintly the position of the lights of a cruise ship and corrected our course in order to get out of its way. Two coast guard boats, only a few hundred meters away, passed us. Again, I corrected our course. Nothing happened.

Suddenly I was startled out of my daydreams. On the right of our boat something long and silvery passed us at high speed and left a fluorescent light. Stefan also saw it and screamed, "careful, there is something."

I thought feverishly: that could have been a torpedo coming from the coastguard boat. Possibly they had seen us. Stefan called out again and pointed to our left. Again something passed us. Instinctively I directed the boat starboard and gave full speed. Then I saw something silvery approach us from the right. I swerved about, and then I had to laugh. I could see clearly the dorsal fin of the supposed torpedo: it was a dolphin. We drew a deep breath. The rest of the trip we were accompanied by a group of four dolphins which obviously went from the coastguard boats to us. They had fun shooting closely past us. The next morning, one of the dolphins jumped so high spirited out of the water that he almost landed on Stefan's lap in our boat.

The dolphins accompanied us as though they were protecting us. The dorsal fins were always visible next to our boat. I had to think about shipwrecked people who were saved by dolphins. Who knows, maybe we would soon need their help.

It was already after midnight when I changed course in the south-eastern direction. Meanwhile we had been traveling eight hours and, according to my calculation, about 90 kilometers. For some time now, I oriented myself on the three stars in the belt of Orion and then on the star Beta Andromeda. With the binoculars I looked at the faintly visible fog of Andromeda, the galaxy that is closest to ours, about two million light years away.

At around three o.clock in the morning we saw the first glimmer of daylight in the East. I got tired and took little cat naps for just a few seconds. Suddenly I heard Stefan's voice who called out something to me. I opened my eyes and realized that the sun had emerged about half way up from the ocean surface. "Look into the sun, there is something!" shouted Stefan.

It was strange — in the center of the red ball of the sun was a small black cross visible. "It could be a sunspot," I answered, but corrected myself immediately: "Nonsense, sunspots could not be seen in this way because of the refraction. Wait a minute; I'll look through my binoculars."

With the binoculars I could immediately see what it was.

"You know what that is? It is a ship, and after that two more. If I am correct, they are traveling in our direction. If that is true, then God help us."

Unfortunately I was right. Half an hour later I saw three warships, one large and two smaller ones, coming directly towards us. Looking at the map I assumed that they were on their way to Burgas, the large harbor of the Bulgarian Black Sea fleet.

The ships went four times as fast as we did. We couldn't possibly avoid them and could only hope that they would go by us at a sufficient distance. With horror we realized that that would not be the case. The large warship approached us continuously as if its finishing line was our boat.

Even if they were not suspicious of our trying to escape, the captain had to take us on board with the assumption we were in distress. We had some West German money and a few compromising papers, which must not get into the hands of the Bulgarian police. As a precaution we had put them in a plastic bag with a stone. If it became critical, we would just toss it overboard. Stefan was ready to do so.

In the meantime the warship was so close and continued its path towards us. I switched the motor off. We lied down in the boats until our bodies were almost under the splash board of the canoe. With the binoculars I watched the deck of the ship which was armed with cannons and rocket launchers. Some sailors ran around on deck. The ship came within 100 meters from us and, to our greatest astonishment, passed north of us at full speed.

"Stefan, this is odd. They should have seen us."

Even in this risky situation Stefan had to joke around: "Maybe they are on exercises to catch some CIA agents on high sea. With mere mortals like us fleeing, they don't bother."

"I rather believe that they called over the radio one of the smaller boats."

The other ships went at different distances past us. A few minutes later they changed their course and turned west to Burgas. We breathed in deeply and crawled out from our hiding place.

Shortly thereafter, we went south-east. My apprehension that they had called seaplane was quickly ousted from my mind. As if the dolphins foresaw the danger we were in, they were gone for a while. After the warships had gone, they reappeared close to our boat and accompanied us due south.

By now, it was day time and we realized that we were far out in the sea. We could not even see the coast. For the first time I had an uneasy feeling; the calmness and the security I had felt in the quiet night under the clear sky was gone. What would happen if a storm came up or the motor stopped? As if on cue, the motor stopped. I tried to restart several times, but without success. We realized rather quickly that the only problem was dirt that kept the spark plug from functioning. After a while we continued.

Around noon the waves got noticeably higher, the wind freshened up. A band of clouds in the West could be seen on the horizon. That was not good news. We knew that clouds above the Black Sea always meant bad weather and strong winds.

We decided to just stay the course. I studied the map. We were on the way for 24 hours and had probably traversed 200 kilometers.

In the early afternoon, the wind got stronger and the waves reached considerable heights, but were not dangerous yet for our boat, since the waves were not only high but also long. But water got into the boat. Initially, that was not a problem, we had a tin with us and we could scoop the water out with it.

But that worked well for only a short time. The waves grew higher and higher and more water got into the boat. Stefan scooped as fast as he could, but realized that it would soon be useless. The water level rose constantly. Soon we would sit in water, and the boat could only stay afloat with the help of the air bubbles in its front and back.

Then I had the saving idea. I loosened the hose of the motor's cooling pump from the outside and brought it into the boat. Now the motor was pumping out the water. Soon the water level sank. Relieved, Stefan put the tin down. For now the danger was gone.

But our concern was the clouds growing more and more in the Western sky. It looked like a major storm might be imminently approaching. The waves now reached heights of two meters and more. I began to doubt the success of our venture. Finally, we decided to go back in the direction of the coast. After so many hours fighting against the waves, our priority was a safe return to land, whether it was in Bulgaria or in Turkey. How absurd and insignificant the Iron Curtain seemed in comparison to the towering waves coming into the boat.

I navigated not directly to the West but remained on a south-west course. Around five in the afternoon I saw the first mountains through my binoculars. I turned my attention to a large bay; north of it I saw a valley, which presumably permitted a river flowing into the sea. I looked at the map, and hope grew. Maybe we had gotten further south than originally thought, which of course was possible due to wind and currents. It might even be the Bay of Bosporus. And from there it was not far to our destination — Istanbul.

Going Ashore at Igneada

I showed the map to Stefan; he was skeptical. In his opinion we were not yet beyond the critical point of our trip — the point where our itinerary crossed the borderline between Bulgaria and Turkey. Indeed, with the minute details of the coastline, it was almost impossible to know our position. According to the map there were several larger bays and also river valleys.

The waves became more and more ominous, so we decided to take course directly towards the coast. At that time we were almost 30 kilometers away from land. I made sure we went due west. Since it was impossible to reach the beach unharmed with our folding canoe because of the large sand dunes, I took course towards what looked like a river valley on the horizon. Should there really be a river flowing into the sea, it would be relatively easy to go into the mouth of the river and then onto land.

We now had to fight against the wind coming from the west. More and more water came into the boat. My trick with the cooling pump was not working anymore and we sat in water up to our hips. I had to admire our boat's stability. It cleared a path through the waves like a submarine gliding on the surface of the water. The motor ran unswervingly although it was spilled over by water from time to time.

In the evening we reached the vicinity of the coast. The sun disappeared behind the mountains. I constantly aimed our course towards the supposed mouth of the river. Meanwhile, the details of the coast became recognizable and the bay further south was visible. I still hoped it was the mouth of the Bosporus. But Stefan kept insisting on his opinion that we still had the Bulgarian coast in front of us.

A few kilometers on this side of the beach, our companions — the dolphins, made a few bold jumps. It was their way of saying goodbye, and after that, they were gone. Our companions were obviously of the opinion that we could fend for ourselves from now on. So close to the coast, nothing probably would happen.

The twilight was quickly upon us. With the binoculars I saw on a hill north of the valley something that looked like a watchtower. We were about 300 meters away from the beach. I was not mistaken; we were indeed at the mouth of a small river.

At that moment Stefan called out, "Down, put your head down!"

Instinctively, I ducked down under the dashboard. A bright spotlight was gliding above us across the water and came back into our faces. Suddenly I realized where we had to be. I had memorized the map of this region and knew that the Iron Curtain ended at this river. To be precise: north of the Bay of Igneada, named after a small Turkish village at the North Coast. Since, according to my estimate, we should have been much further south, I did not think of the possibility of getting to the coast at exactly that spot.

We realized what a catastrophic situation we were in. Without knowing, we had gone many kilometers between the Bulgarian and Turkish borderline towards the coast. The two brothers from the Erzgebirge Mountains, who were killed by Bulgarian grenades not far from here, came to mind.

The spotlight returned once more above the water, and then vanished. Maybe we were lucky and they did not see us. We tried to duck further down into the boat, which was filled with more and more water and looked more like a submarine. Only our heads and the motor were still above the water level. Even for a marksman we would not have been an easy target due to the movement of the strong waves.

I again studied the map. We had to be just at, or very close to, the borderline. That was the only way to explain the appearance of the spotlight. I aimed the boat towards the south-east in order to get some distance from the coast. I went at full speed; the boat was gliding quickly over the waves.

We observed the beach. It was almost dark and we could only see a few details of a tree-covered coast. Near the coast, the waves were reduced in size. We continued south for several hours, keeping a distance of about 200 meters from the coast. It would have been safer to be further out to the sea to protect us from possible exposure to firing by the border police from the coast. But out there, the waves were now much higher and we did not want to take any chance with so much water already in the boat. We saw a blinking beacon in the south, and I aimed the boat towards it.

At about midnight, we finally reached the bay we had seen hours ago. We had calmed down in the meantime, and I became more optimistic. Maybe we were totally wrong and the border was further to the north. That meant that this bay could be indeed the Bay of Bosporus. Stefan doubted my sanity and kept insisting that we were still in Bulgaria.

After the strain of the last hours we were totally exhausted. In front of us I recognized the weak navigation lights of an old sailboat, which passed us with creaking masts like the ghost ship in Richard Wagner's opera "The Flying Dutchman". Presumably there was a harbor close by. We were now determined to go directly into the bay. Lights from a village were visible at the horizon.

Another half an hour later, going against the waves, we could not possibly be far from the beach. A sudden noise made me look back — too late. A huge wall of water came upon us and buried us completely, tipping over the boat. We were thrown out and swept on to the sand. Because of the darkness, we had not seen that we were so close to the beach. A breaker took our boat and tipped it.

Totally exhausted, we crawled onto the shore. After sitting for such a long time, we had to learn to use our legs again. Now our boat followed us by being also washed ashore. We pulled it in with our remaining strength. The journey across the sea had ended after 33 hours.

With a flashlight we looked around and picked up our things that had fallen out of the boat. Luckily it was not much as the plastic cover had protected what was below. Then we tried to figure out what to do next. In any case, we would have to play vacationers from Varna who ran aground, at least as long as we did not know whether we were in Turkey or still in Bulgaria.

We changed our clothes. Luckily, we had packed some of them in plastic bags and they were still dry. Finally, I started exploring the beach. I did not get very far. I heard a voice and looked straight into the beams of a flashlight. A soldier was standing in front of me with a submachine gun pointed at me.

I asked him if he spoke Russian, "Goworite pa russki?". An unintelligible sentence followed and the soldier aimed his gun higher which made me instinctively raise my hands. I became more hopeful since every Bulgarian border patrol would speak at least a few words in Russian. But he did not give the impression that he understood. I continued to speak Russian and asked him to follow me. Only when I accompanied my words with gestures did the soldier understand what I wanted. So we both went back to the place we had come ashore. Astonished he looked at the place with his flashlight and shook his head when he saw the boat and our things spread out.

Stefan unfolded his map and put it on the sand under the light of the flashlight. With gestures we tried to get the soldier to show us where we were. He pointed to the Bay of Igneada, south of the border.

"Igneada?" asked Stefan.

The soldier nodded and pointed to the lights of the village not far from here: "Igneada".

In that second we realized that we were in Turkey, about 20 kilometers south of the Iron Curtain. The simple word "Igneada" sounded like music to our ears. It was synonymous with "rescue". It was the Turkish–Bulgarian border where we had seen the beacons.

"Igneada," Stefan called out again, radiant with joy, and hugged the Turkish soldier, kissed him on both checks and danced on the beach. The soldier was perplexed, said something unintelligible and ran away.

Only a few moments later we were surrounded by soldiers. An officer approached us and welcomed us in broken German. Soon after that we sat in a military barrack close by. It turned out that we were in the middle of a restricted area of the Turkish military. Some of the officers gave us a short interrogation, but it was more like a friendly conversation.

We told them that we came from East Germany and that we traveled from Varna across the Black Sea, and that our final destination would be West Germany. At first they did not believe that we had traveled such a long way from Varna in our small folding canoe, all the way to Igneada. When we explained how we went on the open sea towards the south, close to the coast, along the borderline, they let us know that our lives amounted to very little because, only a few meters north of here, we would have been in the area of the Bulgarian defense, and that would have had fatal consequences.

Finally, they made some phone calls with their army headquarters in Kirklareli; only then were we able to get the well-deserved rest. Of course, neither Stefan nor I could sleep in spite of the exhaustion. We were so excited about our experiences in the past hours.

The following morning the soldiers gave us a very good breakfast. After that they told us that a jeep would take us to Kirklareli. The commander apologized that he had to blindfold us on that trip because foreigners were not allowed to see the military layout at the border.

Stefan and I had heard that the Turkish border police sometimes send refugees back to Bulgaria. Was that perhaps our destination? Maybe that was the reason why they had blindfolded us.

But, considering the friendly way we were treated, I doubted that. But I did remain skeptical. We decided that in case we were transported back to the border we would try to escape or, at least make a lot of noise. When we were driven away in a jeep I was able to lift my blindfold just enough to see with the help of the shadow which the morning sun projected, that we were driving in a south-westerly direction, in any case, not to the north. That gave me a breath of relief.

After a while our blindfolds were taken off. At about noon we arrived at Kirklareli where we were put up at the police station in the center of town.

Istanbul

In Kirklareli we stayed in a pleasantly large room, guarded around the clock by an armed soldier. We were not allowed to go into the city. We were interrogated several times by officers and civilian personnel; we found out soon enough, that their main interest was to find out whether we had any connections to Soviet atomic research institutions. That we came from East Germany did not interest them. When I told them that I had spent some time in Moscow and in Leningrad (today St Petersburg) as a student, they became alert and asked for details.

They also asked us to make a list of all our relatives we had in West Germany: their names and their birthdays. In contrast to Stefan, I had a lot of relatives in West Germany, but, of course, had no idea of their birth dates. They could not believe that I did not know the birthdays of my aunts and uncles. When they repeated their questions regarding birthdays, I just made up some dates — and that did it.

When the officer who had lived in West Germany many years ago and had worked as a guest worker there, looked over the list of my relatives, he saw the name of my uncle: Dr Knorr, a food chemist from Nuremberg. He showed it to his colleagues and they whispered for a while. I heard them mention the name Knorr several times, and then he said, "I know the name of Dr Knorr very well; he produces soups and things like that very well. He has a very big company."

Both of them looked at me appreciatively. I realized only then that they had mistaken my relative for the well-known soup manufacturer. I said nothing, and from then on I was treated extremely cordially, like a guest of honor.

They examined our luggage carefully, especially a book which I had brought along. It was a textbook about elementary particle physics by the Swedish physicist Gunnar Kaellen. It was not so much the book itself, but the fact that it was written in Russian. We assumed that the Turks suspected that the book had secrets about Soviet nuclear physics research. They could not care less when I told them that this textbook was already published years ago in the United States. They believed this to be an important object.

After two days of detention in Kirklareli we were told that we would be brought to Istanbul the next morning. We requested to contact the West German Consulate, but were initially not allowed to do so. The next morning a small truck took us and our luggage, including the folding canoe, to Istanbul.

We observed with great interest how the truck managed to clear a path through the incredible traffic mess of the Turkish capital city. We stopped at a larger house, which turned out to be a police hotel. Our things were brought to our room by soldiers. This room was to be our "home" for the following days. They posted a soldier with a machine gun in front of the room to guard us. We quickly realized that the guard did very little. He smiled at us in a friendly manner and greeted us with "How are you?" We could come and go as we pleased.

In the afternoon we were taken to the police headquarters for another round of interrogation. Again, the same questions about our escape, which we had answered many times before.

The following day we were asked about our religion. I told them that I was by family tradition a Protestant. This answer was received favorably. Stefan could not say anything of that sort since he was without religion. The interrogating officer became suspicious. He asked whether he was a good, positive person.

Stefan asked what a good person was. He was told that only a religious person could be a good person. People without a religion are communists, and communists are all bad. Stefan had no religion; therefore he was obviously a communist.

Stefan and I had to laugh, which was a mistake. Our interrogators looked at us gravely and withdrew for a consultation. Shortly thereafter we were brought back to our hotel. On the way there we passed a shop which interested us. It was a shop that sold nothing else but copies of the head of Kemal Ataturk. Hundreds of Ataturk heads in all sizes. It was a curious sight.

"I saw a shop in Leningrad where you could buy nothing but heads of Lenin." Stefan turned to our companion who spoke a little German and said that the parallel aspects between Lenin and Ataturk were striking. Again, that was something we had better not said. To mention the national hero Ataturk in the same vein as Lenin was a gaffe.

Needless to say, that gaffe came up the next day at the police headquarters. They let us know that I could probably leave for West Germany, but not Stefan who was obviously a communist and his situation was more complicated.

That did it for us, we had had enough. That afternoon we said goodbye to the guard with the usual "How are you?", and left. We took a taxi which brought us to the West German Consulate. When we told the person on duty that we were from Leipzig he could not believe it. "From where?" he asked. "From Leipzig?" he continued, "And you came by boat?"

He shook his head and took us to the consul. Shortly thereafter, the consulate was called by the police headquarters. The Turkish authorities had noticed that we had vanished and they knew where we had gone. There was a small diplomatic complication, but the consul was able to take care of it quickly. A car from the West

German consulate got our things from the hotel and we were put up in the house of a German priest on the premises of the consulate in Istanbul. The consul promised the Turkish authorities that we would be available in the next few days and to place ourselves at the disposal of the authorities for further questioning. He made us aware that from now on, we would be under the protection of the West German Consulate. This was only reluctantly accepted by the Turkish authorities.

In the following days we were driven several times in a company car of the consulate to police headquarters for questioning. After the initial difficulties, we now had an almost friendly relationship with the officers. They even tried to talk us into staying in Turkey. There were always positions for physicists at the universities. We thanked them but declined their offer. One officer mentioned that the Turkish girls were much better and more beautiful than the German girls. Finally they promised to settle our situation quickly so that we could get our exit visas soon.

On the second day of our stay as guests in the beautiful villa of the priest, our host brought the newest edition of the Istanbul daily paper, the "Cumhyriet". On page 2 we could read the exact details of our escape and our personal data. Our arrival in Igneada was written in an emotional way. The paper even added an interview with the soldier Stefan had hugged and kissed. The journalists did not forget to mention that we had with us secret materials about the Soviet nuclear research in Russian, which was translated into Turkish. It was the book by Kaellen.

It was probably the first and only time that the Turkish secret police had parts of a physics textbook translated from Russian into Turkish. I decided to inform Gunnar Kaellen about this after our arrival in West Germany. Unfortunately, I had no opportunity to do so, because Kaellen died in October 1968 in a plane crash on his way from Geneva to Sweden. The plane crashed near Hannover during an emergency landing.

The article in the Cumhyriet had resulted the West German newspapers reporting about our escape in the following day. And in this way, the East German secret police found out, much earlier than anticipated by us, about our escape. Also the Bulgarian authorities found out through these articles about the unusual route we took in order to get away. As we later heard, their security system at the border of the Black Sea coast had changed after our escape. A few of the security officers had to bear the responsibility for our successful escape.

We were astonished to hear from the consulate staff that, until then, no one was ever successful in escaping from Bulgaria by boat. There were no data available about unsuccessful attempts.

We were spending very relaxed days in Istanbul. Our hosts, the consulate staff and the employees of Lufthansa were extremely helpful. The consul gave us the consulate car with a chauffeur at our disposal. We were able to do some sightseeing in the old city of Istanbul and its surroundings. We came to know the picturesque Bazaar, and we were also able to take excursions to the Asian side of the city and to the beach islands. Both the consulate and the Lufthansa office organized a welcome party for us, inviting all Germans living in Istanbul.

Ten days after our arrival in Turkey, on Tuesday, August 6, 1968, an employee of the consulate brought us to the airport where we boarded a Lufthansa plane to Munich. In the late morning the plane left the Istanbul airport, which is located directly by the sea. Stefan and I sat silently and we looked down from our seats onto the Yugoslavian Adria coast as it slowly passed below us. We were both thinking about our future in an unknown country to which we now flew. We landed in the afternoon at the Munich-Riem airport. A new period in our lives would begin.

The Years Thereafter

A few days after my arrival in West Germany I telephoned from Frankfurt to my parents. My mother thought I called from Frankfurt-at-the-Oder. It took a while for her to realize that I was calling from the West. We only had a few seconds before our conversation was interrupted by the monitoring service of the secret police. But at least my parents now knew that I had escaped and was safe. Fortunately, my parents did not have problems with the authorities. My father was self-employed. Had he been working as an employee in a state-owned company, he would have had massive problems.

From October 1968 on, I worked at the Max Planck Institute for Physics in Munich, which was directed by Werner Heisenberg. In 1970 I went to the United States to work at the Stanford Linear Accelerator Center (SLAC) of Stanford University. I started to collaborate with Murray Gell-Mann, who had just gotten the Nobel Prize in Physics and was based at the California Institute of Technology (Caltech) in Pasadena close to Los Angeles. I commuted every two weeks between SLAC and Caltech, until I left the US in March 1971 and returned to the Max Planck Institute. In November 1971 I received my PhD at the Technical University in Munich. From September 1971 I worked at CERN in Geneva, Switzerland where I collaborated again with Murray Gell-Mann who was spending a year there.

Stefan went to Hamburg after the escape in order to get his PhD in philosophy under Carl Friedrich von Weizsaecker. Later he worked on philosophical questions and followed Weizsaecker to his new Institute in Starnberg near Munich.

In spite of all the efforts of the Secret Police, they did not find out any details about our role in the "subversive" action in Leipzig for a long time. The details were never found out by the Secret Police. About one year after our escape they discovered that Stefan and I had something to do with the transparency and its placement in the Leipzig Congress Hall. This information got to them, very likely, through an East German spy in Munich. That Stefan never revealed the name of Rudolf Treumann as the one who painted the transparency, paid off. The secret police never found out. Treumann escaped to the West much later with the help of friends in West Germany. Today, he works at the Max Planck Society in a research facility in Garching near Munich.

To this day, it remains unclear whether the heart attack of Paul Froehlich had anything to do with the transparency action. In support of this assumption we might point to the fact that several people in Leipzig were put in jail because of the protest action in the Congress Hall, although nobody could prove they had anything to do with it. The Secret Police needed to appear strong and unfailing in front of the state's leadership, so they had to force confessions out of people.

Because of their political activities and the suspicion that they had tried to flee in 1971, i.e. three years after our escape, quite a few of our friends and acquaintances, including my cousin Guenter Fritzsch and Lothar Hill, were taken into custody and put in jail for some time. This was one of many inexcusable acts of the East German regime. Although Lothar and Guenter had not been active in the transparency action at the Congress Hall, it played an important role in the interrogations. The Secret Police were obviously interested in playing this event up.

Guenter was released from prison in late 1972 and he had to work as a physicist in the Leipzig telephone exchange. He was not allowed to continue his research in biophysics at Leipzig University. A few years later he came to West Germany legally. Today he is a biophysicist at the Max Planck Institute at Frankfurt.

Lothar Hill was allowed to go to West Germany in 1972 after his incarceration. Today, he is working for a church organization in Baden-Wuerttemberg.

On August 21, 1968, two weeks after our arrival in West Germany, the armies of the Warsaw Pact marched into Czechoslovakia. For Susanne's mother, who had strong family ties to Prague and always showed great interest in the development of the "Prague Spring", this, together with the stress from her job, was too much for her. She had a massive heart attack and needed to be taken care for over a year. Susanne interrupted her studies at the university in order to take care of her mother.

We exchanged several coded letters in which I asked her to come to West Germany. I would have organized an escape via Czechoslovakia. I received letters from her, in which I saw how much she wrestled with herself. Finally she told me that the health of her mother would not allow her to leave East Germany. With that, our relationship basically ended. At the beginning of 1970s she married a lecturer from the Technical University in Dresden. They now have a daughter. Today, Susanne is a medical doctor and director of a children's clinic near Dresden.

I met my wife Brigitte the year after my escape in Munich, where she was a student. We got married in 1971.

In 1977, almost nine years after my escape, my father died at age 72. I was working in Geneva at the time. I called the East German lawyer Vogel to find out if I could attend the funeral in Zwickau. Vogel, who was well versed in inner German problems, told me unequivocally, "Absolutely not." Even as an employee of CERN, an international organization, I would be arrested immediately. Only my wife was allowed to attend the funeral.

The large conference in my special field of elementary particle physics, which happens every two years, was to be held in the United States in 1982. And the one in 1984 was to be held in the Soviet Union. In the early 80s the diplomatic relations between the Soviet Union and the United States and West European countries were at a low point due to the invasion in Afghanistan. It was a fact that the American and the West European physicists did not want to have the meeting in the Soviet Union. The Russian physicists knew this and suggested as an alternative: Leipzig, Budapest or Belgrade.

At a meeting in Bonn in 1981, I met Professor Herwig Schopper, the director-general of CERN in Geneva. He told me that Leipzig had a good chance of holding the conference in 1984, if some problems would be removed by that time.

"What problems would that be?" I asked curiously,

"Well, for one thing, the authorities would have to give the physicists from Israel who wanted to come visas to enter the country. And right now that is not certain. In addition, there are other unresolved cases, like your case. If they do not give you a visa, Leipzig as the conference city would be out of the question."

"When will that be decided?"

"The meeting will be next Tuesday."

"Does that mean that I probably have to go to Leipzig?"

"Have to — is exaggerated," Schopper said and laughed. "I would say that you have a certain obligation to go. Anyway, if I were you, I would go. This opportunity doesn't come again so soon."

"You know that I am on certain lists of the Secret Police. I fall under an amnesty regarding my escape, but the political protest action I took at the time was never pardoned."

"I spoke with the delegation from East Germany about your case," reported Schopper. "They assured me that there wouldn't be any problems, and I believe them. There will be about a thousand physicists coming to Leipzig from different Western countries. If they would arrest you, even just for a few hours, there would be a strongly worded protest. The conference would be cancelled. East Germany cannot afford that. But I would suggest that you leave that East Germany before the end of the conference. That is to ensure that the Secret Police doesn't do anything stupid after the end of the conference." "Good idea," I said, "but let's first wait and see what the result will be on Tuesday."

The next Tuesday, Schopper told me that Leipzig was chosen, and also, that I would have no problems entering East Germany.

At the beginning of 1984 I received an invitation to the Leipzig conference. A few weeks later I applied for a visa from the East German administration. The visa was granted quickly.

The research ministry in Bonn told me that there would be absolutely no problem with my going to Leipzig and actually encouraged me to go to the conference. Also, the official of the Munich State Chancellery told me to go ahead, but advised me to stay in contact with the appropriate authorities during my travels, just in case. In this way, any potential interference from the East German side could be brought to the attention of the Bavarian government.

Back in East Germany

"Remember, you are still driving through Germany."

The sign at the Autobahn (freeway) from Nuernberg to Berlin informs the drivers that they were getting closer to the border into East Germany. At the last rest place along the Autobahn west of the border, I telephoned the secretary of Franz Josef Strauss, the head of the government in Bavaria, and told her that within a few minutes I would be in East Germany.

"Well, keep going as we planned it," she answered. "Have a good journey. I am looking forward to our next conversation a week from now."

After another call to my wife in Munich, I examined my papers, and I was happy that all necessary documents were there: passport, personal documents, my invitation to the conference. the "counting documents" that was needed to cross the border, and the custom's document. I drove back onto the Autobahn and passed the last checkpoint. At the end of the bridge, I saw the first border stigmata — barriers, guard posts and a fence. I drove within the speed limit of 30 kilometers per hour. I passed the formal barrier, passing two border guards who appeared to be chatting without paying any attention to me. A couple of minutes later, the customs officer looked at my documents.

In the local dialect he said, "So, you were born in Zwickau, and you are now driving to Leipzig. Well, have a nice drive and a pleasant stay." He didn't bother to look at my luggage in the trunk and gave me a sign to move on.

There were only a few miles left before the exit to Schleiz was indicated. I watched carefully the cars behind me: two vehicles with Berlin license plates passed me; there was no indication that anybody was following me. I exited the freeway and took the country road in the direction of Plauen. From there I got on the freeway to Zwickau. The conference was to begin the day after, in Leipzig, and I had planned to spend the night at my parents' home.

At noon I arrived at my hometown of Reinsdorf — which is just a couple of miles outside of Zwickau — without any interference. My mother, my sister and my two brothers were expecting me. They planned to celebrate my first visit home after 16 years.

On Thursday, July 19, 1984, the conference started in Leipzig. In the early morning I entered the city in my car from the southeast, near the big war memorial. I had not been there for 16 years, but nothing seemed to have changed. All over, the East German scenery that I had traversed looked unchanged. It looked as if nothing had happened in all these years. I just had the impression that things were paler and greyer than I had remembered. But maybe that was just a first, subjective impression.

I continued towards the town center, to St John's Square, and I was looking forward to seeing what Karl-Marx Square would look like with its new construction, after the destruction of the church and the university. My old landlady Frau Hempel had sent me postcards showing the new city center, so I knew more or less what to expect. But the reality was much worse than the photo image on the postcard I had seen.

On Karl-Marx Square I stepped on my brakes so suddenly that the driver behind me honked his horn furiously. After all, he could not possibly imagine that what I now faced hit me like a tremendous blow. Where previously the university with its facade, designed by Schinkel, had been standing next to the church, I now saw nothing but a hideous grey concrete block, and to the left of it an ostentatious high rise, which was called by the people "the professor's launching pad". Those buildings were barely 15 years old, but looked old. So this was what had happened to the square, of which Paul Froehlich had announced that this square would be the most beautiful square in Europe.

I continued my drive to the Merkur Hotel. I knew that it was the best hotel in Leipzig and also excellently guarded. After checking in, I tried to find any evidence of surveillance in my room, but without success. I should not have been astonished, since the hotel had been built by a Japanese firm, and it was evidently equipped with the most up-to-date electronic devices. It turned out that after the fall of the Berlin wall in November 1989, they found in the basement of the hotel an excellently equipped electronic listening device.

In the afternoon, I finally checked in with the conference organization. Professor Lanius from East Berlin, whom I had met at several scientific meetings, came to say hello. He was the chief organizer of this conference, and he came daily to ask me whether I felt the meeting was going well. He asked me to tell him about any problems I might notice.

On the second day of the conference, during the lunch break, I drove to Stoetteritz, after driving aimlessly through the Leipzig center to be sure that no one was following me. I was going to find out soon that these cautionary measures were not without good reason.

Looking at the part of the city I had lived in, I realized that nothing had changed either. I thought that East Germany was a country where time was lost. Taking a closer look, I realized that the houses appeared more run down than years before, including Holstein Strasse 26 where I had lived. And in no time flat, my former landlady, Mrs Hempel, being now in her late 80s and hardly changed during all that time, appeared. It took her a while to realize that I was truly back after all these years. We drank coffee together and had a good, long talk. In spite of her age, Mrs Hempel was still in fairly good shape. Just as in all those past years, she hosted two students in her apartment, not least to add a bit to her very modest pension.

"Should I tell you, Harald, how little I get from the state? I get all of 350 Marks. They call it the minimum old age support; hunger pension I call it, and I am supposed to live on that. They give much more to the young people now, but not to us old people. They think we should quickly disappear, either to the cemetery or to West Germany. This is the last patriotic action which the government and the party want to see us perform. But I'll show them, I'll stick around until I'm 100 years old or more!"

I told Mrs Hempel some details of my escape to the West, which she did not know, and of its motivations, like the story of the transparency.

"You recall, Harald, how we, after the concert, drank to the health of the creator of the transparency," she recalled. "My God, had I only known that you played an important part in it. But I am sure that it was better that you didn't tell me. In the end, the Secret Police could have found out. You should have seen them sniff around your room here after they heard about your escape. Afterwards your room looked as if a bomb had exploded inside. And then they wanted to leave without putting some order to the place. I told them: No. Only if they would take me away right away, I told them and stood in front of the door. That was when the youngsters gave up, not older than 25 years old. They could have been my grandchildren. You should have seen how nicely they put your room back in order."

There was a big reception for the participants of the conference in the evening. That provided me the opportunity to see many of my previous fellow students, who by this time had been scattered all over East Germany. When I talked to friends or acquaintances I was cautious. I had to watch out for the Secret Police, who no doubt were at the reception. My conjecture was correct. After the conference I heard from Leipzig that about 30 of those "security" agents had been there.

During the reception, a good acquaintance, Professor Salam, who was the director of the International Center for Theoretical Physics in Trieste, came up to me and pulled me to a corner for a long talk. Salam had gotten the Nobel Prize in physics five years ago and had been busy exploiting the prestige of that distinction to garner additional support for his institute, which was supported by UNESCO. At the conference he had explored with several East German colleagues the possibilities of providing some physicists with a chance to visit his institute in Trieste. And in this way he could improve international contacts. And since the necessary means were not available, he asked me to talk to the Department of Inner-German affairs in Bonn.

I promised to help, but pointed out that this department might not be the correct place. I knew that this institute in Bonn along with the West German Intelligence Service was a red flag for the East German government. East German scientists were strictly forbidden to receive financial support to travel in West Germany or to other Western countries from this source.

As our conversation came to an end, I noticed that a few meters from us was a man leaning against pillar, apparently with no relation to us. His right arm was bent in an upward angle that could not be overlooked. Weeks later I found out that our conversation had been recorded by means of a microphone. This man had been a member of the Secret Police.

Trying to understand the conversation, no doubt, astonished the Secret Police people, who clearly had expected something else. There I was, an "enemy of the communist state", talking to

Professor Salam in the Leipzig City Hall and trying to find ways to help East German physicists to establish contacts with Western countries, aided by subsidies of a West German department.

Late in the evening, I walked out of City Hall together with Professor Eberhard Zeidler, a good acquaintance who, by this time, had managed to overcome considerable difficulties and obtain a professorship of mathematics in Leipzig. In the early 1960s, when he was probably the most promising mathematics student in Leipzig, he had refused to support the building of the wall facing West Germany. He was suspended from his studies and was forced into strenuous physical labor due to his action. Only three years later he was permitted to return to his studies. He was remarkably qualified and persistent, and finally wound up obtaining a professorship.

Eberhard Zeidler and I wandered through the downtown streets for quite a while and exchanged memories of the past, and discussed our scientific interests. It was quite late by this time; the streetcars operated only rarely at such late hours, and I drove him home in my car. We made a dinner appointment for the next day in his apartment. Only then did I notice that my car was being followed by a blue Wartburg car all the way to the hotel's parking lot.

The next morning Eberhard walked up to me and said, "You know what; there is a problem with respect to our planned get-together. I had people coming to see me this morning — I needn't tell you who. Quite obviously we were watched last night. I was told that any further contact with you would be harmful. I need not tell you what that might mean for me. Anytime I want to go abroad, I need a permit. Those guys could mean real trouble for me."

I nodded and agreed that it would not be wise to take a risk in this context.

"But our planned dinner appointment we will have, even if it'll be a few years from now, when all this nonsense will have stopped here. Or we'll get together for dinner in Munich."

He laughed heartily and slapped me on the shoulder saying, "You are quite an optimist. Let's do just as you said."

On Sunday evening I met Susanne and her husband Georg in the Japanese restaurant at the Merkur-Hotel. They had come to Leipzig just for that purpose. My escape from East Germany was now 16 years ago. Neither of us would have expected to meet again. The woman whom I had loved as a young student was now a very attractive lady who knew who she was and what she could do.

We talked about our families. I showed her photos of my wife and my two sons, taken during a Mediterranean vacation. Susanne conveyed greetings from her mother, who lived in her house in Dresden. She then brought me up to date on her professional development since those student times in Leipzig and told me about her clinical activities. And finally we talked about what had happened when I managed to escape from East Germany; also, about the transparency action and what happened after that.

Georg talked about the troubles he encountered at Dresden University looking for a teaching position while not being a member of the communist party. Ever since the mid-1960s, all teaching jobs at the East German universities were assigned according to political criteria. Academic qualification counted, if at all, only in a secondary way.

I pointed out to Susanne and Georg that our get-together was likely to be watched by the Secret Police agents. Susanne did not seem to be fazed by that. "I'm quite sure that these people want to find out with whom you are in contact here," she said, "but we couldn't care less. We're not living in 1968 anymore. Georg and I know we have been sharply watched for years. I am sure that my telephone line in the clinic is under surveillance. But we are no longer afraid — that's what's new. They don't throw people in jail anymore as they did years ago. Georg and I are working to improve things, and we'll not be discouraged. After all, what can they do? Georg accepted, years ago, that he wouldn't get a professorial position due to his refusal to become a member of the communist party, or to work for the Secret Police. I myself am not shy to say what I think. They cannot take away my job as a medical doctor. I take advantage of the fact that doctors are in high demand."

"I have never been to the West, but I often think of how things must be there," Georg mused. "Here in East Germany we're all sitting in one and the same boat, and everyone helps his neighbor to somehow survive the disgraceful circumstances of our lives, which we know only too well. There isn't much here in East Germany that can be admired, but I am impressed at times with the solidarity among people. Not that I have illusions: we want this country to become free sometime soon, that all the pressure on us will vanish. Not only must some new arrangement push all of the old pressure out, but something new and independent will have to appear. I consider that development our most important task."

"Let's just hope that your dreams will come true soon," I said. "There must be an end to all this. The regime will collapse like a house of cards. And I do hope it will happen in this decennium."

"You have not given up being the optimist you were long ago," Susanne said. "It will take a long time. Give up your dream of the future!"

"I'm sure you know 'The Plague' by Albert Camus: one day the plague had vanished all of a sudden, and a new wind blew from the ocean, and the city regenerated. That is what will happen here. The house of cards will collapse, and people will ask themselves why it took so long."

"I hope you are right, although for right now, I cannot believe it."

It had gotten late when we left the restaurant. I accompanied Susanne and Georg to the railroad station. Nobody was following us.

The last days of the conference, Monday to Wednesday, were taken up by the big plenary sessions. Those were held in the Congress Hall, where 16 years earlier, we had managed to execute the transparency action. The big hall had barely changed since 1968.

During the first presentation that morning, I was barely able to concentrate on its content. I closed my eyes and relived in my thoughts what had happened on that concert evening in 1968. I saw the rapid unrolling of the big yellow transparency and the following thunderous applause of the Leipzig citizens.

A California friend of mine observed me and walked up to me during the intermission, and said, "I see you had problems concentrating on the talk. I can imagine why. Do you recall that we talked years ago, in my house, about the transparency that you unrolled here? Come on, let's go to the stage, I want to see how you did it at that time."

A few minutes later, a small group of physicists, mostly from the United States, was standing on the stage of the Congress Hall, and I told them a few details. A colleague from Berkeley started climbing up the ladder that had permitted Stefan Welck to hang the transparency.

The conference was to come to its conclusion on Wednesday. I had prepared for my departure on Tuesday afternoon, because I wanted to spend the next night at my home in Zwickau. At the designated time I exited the city on the main exit road going south, and again, the blue Wartburg car followed me. In the rear view mirror, I saw it stop at a gas station before entering Altenburg. And after that I was left alone. I felt that the Secret Police felt they had done their duty. And less than an hour later I arrived in Reinsdorf without any intervention.

On Wednesday, I had to cross the border into West Germany by 1 pm at the latest. To be on the safe side, I left at nine o'clock in the morning. I reached the border control point to the north of Hof at about 10:30. Another half hour later, I passed the tank barrier. I passed the border patrol and customs without any problems. I heaved a sigh of relief; my travels through East Germany had come to an end.

From the telephone booth at the border, I called the secretary of Strauss and told her that I was coming back and that I would be in Munich around 3 pm. This was about the time the Leipzig conference would end, as planned.

After the Fall of the Wall

In November 1989, I was working at CERN, the European research center in Geneva, Switzerland. I had dinner with colleagues at a hotel in St Genis close to CERN on November 9. Around 10 pm I drove to my apartment in Ferney-Voltaire at the French-Swiss border. Just as I reached the border, I heard from radio that the Berlin Wall had been opened. Tens of thousands of people from East Berlin poured into the Western part of the city. A public festival, as never seen before, began.

I had to think of the courageous citizens of Leipzig who had, only weeks before, shook up the power of the East German regime by demonstrating in various places, including the square that had once been shared by the University and St Paul's Church.

A few minutes later, I arrived at my apartment and turned on the television. What I saw was something that I thought impossible only an hour before. Thousands of East Berlin citizens were climbing over the wall, and the border police stood by and did nothing. As we know today, this day marked the end of the East German Republic. One year later, it no longer existed. Now there was only one unified Germany.

I thought that now was a good time to write a book about the protest action in Leipzig and about our escape. The first edition of this book was published in the fall of 1990.

When I returned from a trip in October 1990, my wife told me that Mrs Weber from Bonn had telephoned several times. That evening she called again. I assumed it was the secretary's office of the minister of research, Mr Riesenhuber, with whom I had spoken by telephone previously.

But on the phone was Mrs Juliane Weber, the private secretary of Helmut Kohl, the chancellor of West Germany at that time. She asked if I could speak to the chancellor now and connected me with Helmut Kohl. He told me that he had received my book from his wife and had begun to read it just the night before. He wanted to read only a few pages; he told me that he was so fascinated by the subject that he had finished the book the same night. He had therefore little sleep and then went to his office very early.

"You know, it is important that you should come to Bonn soon," said Chancellor Kohl. "Tell me when you can come." We agreed to meet the following Friday.

On Friday, October 12, 1990, I flew to Bonn and went directly to the Chancellery. Juliane Weber introduced me to Helmut Kohl. We spoke about the protest action in Leipzig. He was also interested in the technical details of the escape. Finally he said, "Obviously you are one of the few West German scientists who know the former East German Republic. I need your assistance because we have to make important decisions in the near future. I suggest that you form a small commission with whom I can consult. But it has to be done quickly." I agreed and suggested that I would call him again soon.

Our meeting lasted about three hours. We talked about science and universities in the DDR, and later about personal things. Afterwards I went to the Humboldt Foundation and met Heinrich Pfeiffer, secretary-general of the Humboldt Foundation, with whom I intended to discuss the next steps in this matter. I knew Mr Pfeiffer quite well, and I respected his opinions.

I consulted with Pfeiffer and his colleague Dr Hanle about the composition of the small commission. Afterwards, I telephoned the future members which included besides me, Professor Wolf

Lepenies (sociologist at the Free University of Berlin, who had been rector of the scientific college of Berlin from 1986 to 2001); Professor Reimar Luest (astrophysicist and president of the Humboldt Foundation from 1989 to 1999); Professor Benno Parthier (biologist at the University of Halle and president of the German Academy of Science Leopoldina from 1990 to 2003) and Professor Eberhard Stennert (medical professor of the University of Cologne).

The first meeting with Chancellor Kohl was on November 30, 1990. On that morning I picked up Stennert in Cologne and we drove to the chancellery in Bonn, where we met the other members. Chancellor Kohl received us in good spirits and let us to a large table in his office. Although it was only ten in the morning, we were offered a fine wine he had chosen from the Palatinate. We later had lunch in the chancellery's dining room, and in the afternoon we proceeded with our discussions.

To begin with, the talks were about the future of the research facilities of the former East German universities. Kohl was of the opinion that specialized scientists, say, physicists or medical doctors, had nothing to do with East German politics. It should be easy to integrate them into the West German system.

At this point he was met with strong opposition from all members of the commission. True, these scientists had indeed nothing to do with the political doctrines in their special fields; but in order to become professor they had to be loyal to the regime. In time this led to the fact that the best scientists were usually not chosen for the high-up positions. Instead, those who could prove themselves through their political activities besides their scientific qualifications got the best positions. Almost all important positions in science and research were occupied by inferior scientists. Chancellor Kohl's opinion was hard to change, but finally we were able to convince him that all scientists who would work in the unified Germany had to undergo a unified procedure. We proposed: At the end of 1991 all scientists of the former East Germany should step down, and in the beginning of 1992 the good scientists should be rehired. This was, in particular, to be done within the entire field of the Academy of Science.

Since the universities would, in the future, be governed by the federal states, the commission gave a recommendation to the future state governments to act accordingly. Unfortunately, not all state governments kept up with these recommendations. The former Academy of Science had a rather good transformation while the universities changed nothing in the beginning. Some states like Saxony did more and others, like Mecklenburg-Vorpommern, did nothing.

In the year 1990 and 1991, I was a member of a small commission of physicists who were to work out suggestions for the future of the institutes of the Academy. We visited the different institutes relatively quickly and had to give concrete suggestions soon after. Our meetings began in late September 1990 at the ZIE (Central Institute of Electron Physics in East Berlin), which was a large institute for solid state physics.

I still remember the discussions about the future of the Institute for High Energy Physics in Zeuthen in the state of Brandenburg. It appeared that the commission was planning to suggest closure of that institute. But I suggested to tie it to DESY, Hamburg, one of the world's leading research centers using particle accelerators. The commission could not decide, and I was asked to find out if DESY would be at all interested in such a cooperation.

I immediately went to Hamburg and asked Professor Soergel, the director of DESY, and the deputy director Professor Soeding to meet in an Italian restaurant in Othmarschen, a suburb of Hamburg near DESY. I told Soergel about the possibility of incorporating the Zeuthen Institute with DESY (Deutsches Elektronen-Synchrotron). I asked him to think about it and let me know quickly. After the dessert Soergel asked to speak with Soeding alone. I left the table for a few minutes. Afterwards Soergel said that DESY would indeed be interested in a cooperation with the institute in Zeuthen.

Of course, I welcomed this decision and went back to Berlin the next morning. After further discussions the commission decided to combine the two institutes. Today, the Zeuthen Institute DESY Zeuthen is an important part of DESY.

It was difficult for me to decide the future of the Institute for Gravitational Physics of the Academy of Science in Potsdam. In 1968, I had finished my diploma under Professor Hans-Juergen Treder at that institute. Now, I was there in another capacity and I had to decide the future of it. On September 27, 1990, the commission met with the members of that institute, including Professor Treder, in order to discuss the future research there. We decided to close the institute. There was no other alternative since the institute members did not have a convincing scientific program.

Professor Treder resisted and sent out letters all over the world, criticizing the commission's decision. His action was successful. Professor Treder suggested to the recipients of his letter to write directly to Germany's President von Weizsaecker, who intervened by suggesting to close the institute, but then to build a new Institute for Gravitational Physics in the framework of the Max Planck Foundation. Professor Treder's argument could be invalidated this way. Today, the new institute is located in Golm, near Potsdam, and is an important research facility for gravitational problems.

Another case was the future of the Institute in Rossendorf near Dresden, which had been built around a nuclear reactor during the East German era. Since there was no future for the reactor, the question was whether to close the institute or not. I was leaning towards closure, but decided to speak first with Professor Biedenkopf, Prime Minister of the new federal state of Saxony.

I had already met Biedenkopf in the 1980s during the bestowal of an honorary doctorate on the publisher Klaus Piper at Munich

University. Since then we have kept in contact by letters and by telephone. On December 6, 1990, I drove to his office, which was in the former State Security office in Dresden. Biedenkopf pleaded unequivocally for the continuation of the institute in Rossendorf. This was a recommendation which the commission followed.

Another decision had to be made about the Institute for Semiconductor Physics in Frankfurt/Oder. East Germany had created this institute in order to keep up with the development of semiconductor physics in the West. They had been unable to compete with the West, but had the best instruments which had been obtained by illegal methods from the West. A closure of this institute was not an option. We decided that a foreign member of the commission, a professor from Sweden, should be the interim director of the institute.

During our work we also had positive experiences as in the case of Professor Bethge at the Institute for Solid State Physics in Halle. Bethge had guided the institute with high standards for many years and did not allow positions to be filled under political considerations. That led to our decision to keep the institute open in the framework of the Max Planck Society.

Reflections in 2004 — Leipzig Pauliner Society

The reunification of Germany was a dramatic experience for which West Germany was ill prepared. Major mistakes were made by the ruling party, the CDU (Christian Democratic Party) in Bonn after the reunification.

In my opinion, the biggest failure was in matters of the economy. Converting East German money into West German currency in the relation of one to one was certainly a mistake. A relation of two to one would have been more realistic. The conversion had the effect that the pensions in East Germany were too high, given the fact that the people in East Germany had never contributed to the West German pension system.

Another fact was that many people in the former East Germany were put into early retirement in order to get better unemployment statistics. Some people aged 55 were asked to retire, and this was an extreme burden to the social system, which gave out much more money than they had collected, and the taxpayer had to pay the difference. Not only the unemployed in East Germany, but also in the West — in my opinion — received too high an allowance. A friend of mine, who had a dental practice near Leipzig, told me that she was unable to get a cleaning person though in that region the unemployment rate was 25%.

It is distressing to see that some Eastern European countries, such as Poland, solved these problems much better than the new states of Germany. The unemployment rate is much lower there.

In 1990, the people of East Germany were so happy to get rid of the oppressive communist regime that they would have taken on a sizable burden. Instead, they were received by the comfortable social system of West Germany and got wages which were equal to those of the West, but measured in relation to their productivity these wages were much too high; and the expected effects appeared soon. The people in East Germany felt that now was the time for the West Germans to do something to help them. The labor unions supported this way of thinking and demanded equal pay although the productivity was much less in the East. Presumably in a few years the economy in Poland, Czechoslovakia and other Eastern countries will be doing better than the one in East Germany, even though the latter receive large subventions from the West.

In my talks with Chancellor Kohl I often touched on that same topic and pointed out that his government had made serious mistakes. I was unable to convince him of that. He said that mistakes were unavoidable and that West Germany would deal with them. In this case he was wrong, because in the meantime the country encountered great financial problems, a large part of which was due to the reunification.

One grave mistake, in my eyes, was the large tax break given to anybody who was willing to invest in real estate in East Germany. This tax break, strongly supported by the FDP (Free Democratic Party), had the consequence that too many apartment buildings were built. In the end the investor was cheated. Today, many of the new and renovated apartments are empty. Also, West German construction companies started recruiting foreign workers who were cheaper than the ones from East Germany. It would have made more sense if the tax breaks had been less and the work done by East German workers.

But the united Germany is doing rather well, and gradually, in a few years, the consequences of these mistakes will be eradicated. The people of both the West and the East now perceive themselves as citizens of Europe. Here are the new challenges, and chances are good that Germany's citizens will master these challenges.

As early as 1990, Rudolf Treuman, Stefan Welzk and I were accepted as honorary members of the Pauliner Society in Leipzig. The society adopted and followed the words of our transparency: "We demand reconstruction." which Stefan Welzk, Rudolf Treuman and I had chosen for our transparency. St Paul's Church was now supposed to be rebuilt roughly in the shape of the facade built in 1899.

The text on our transparency was not expressing a serious demand — it was simply meant to express our protest. Now I support the demand of the Pauliner Society. In the past, St Paul's Church had played a dual role as a church and as an assembly hall of the university. Such a role would be acceptable for the future.

The majority of the citizens of former East Germany were against the destruction of the church. There were open protests in the days of May 1968, at the time when their southern neighbor established the Prague reform movement. The detonation that demolished the church was therefore a political act in order to stifle any resistance against the East German regime. Ulbricht and his people in Leipzig, who speedily implemented his wishes, did not think that the role of the University Church as a center of the political opposition would just move over to the neighboring St Nikolai Church. It is not an accident that the place of the detonation was the place where 21 years later the power of the government of East Germany was broken.

Some believe that reconstruction would be foolish because the citizens of Leipzig let the detonation happen at that time, although the majority was against it. I think this argument of guilt allocation is questionable; and I would like to point out that thousands of Leipzig citizens went that evening to the cordoned off church shortly before the detonation, in order to bid farewell. One might ask whether continuing protest actions of the people could have prevented the destruction. No one can give a final answer to this question. The fact is that on 23 May 1968, a devious act was played out at the Leipzig city hall. The city counselors, except one, had agreed to go ahead with the destruction, knowing that the majority of the people were against it. Many members of the East German ruling party were also against the detonation but remained silent, although they might not have been exposed to serious penalties, maybe just the loss of some small privilege.

Again, it proved that obedience to authority was considered the most important virtue. Someone who just does what he or she has been told does not shoulder responsibility; this was a customary and convenient opinion. With this sentiment jurists came to terms with working on history without discussing any guilt. This works today as it had worked in Germany in 1945. To render resistance under these conditions may not make sense. Resistance is not exhausted only by conspicuous and dangerous acts. Civil courage is missing in Germany, as is a firm will to walk upright in politically stormy weather. Bismarck once said, "Bravery on the battlefield is with us a common property, but it is not rare, that reputable citizens are lacking civil courage." There are so many examples that show that with bravery and civil courage people can accomplish much, even under dictatorships.

Today, we live in a constitutional state under a free and democratic order, which in West Germany was not gained by working for it, but given as a present by the Western Allies. The citizens of East Germany were not that lucky after World War II; they did not receive such a gift. Only 40 years later did they get freedom and democracy by their own strength; by resisting openly on the square where the detonation took place, in full view of the arriving troops of the East German regime.

Today's constitutional state gives us no guaranty for the future. It can exist only by the cooperation of its citizens who are raised to respect intellectual freedom and independence, and who are willing to make their own decisions and take responsibility for these decisions. They are also expected to resist and not avoid conflicts. Only in tension between civil duties and active resistance is freedom able to develop concretely and be preserved. This is the only way to detect social malformations early on and to correct them.

The reconstruction of the University Church would mean that the citizens of Leipzig take responsibility for the restoration of the cultural identity of their city. Leipzig has been a symbol in Europe since 1989. The shaping of the most important square of the city has its own symbolic effect. Faint-heartedness has no place here. Only those who think big can accomplish big things. The university needs a worthy assembly hall in the shape of St Paul's Church.

Surely, reconstruction needs money; but the means are being invested and not immediately used. Whoever believes, that investments in culture, art and science are a luxury, is wrong. These investments in our time are measured in the future. They determine the moral and mental strength of our time, and therewith the readiness to meet critical developments forcefully and courageously in the future.